EVERYDAY ANGELS

ANNETTE SMITH

HARVEST HOUSE PUBLISHERS
Eugene, Oregon 97402

Cover by Left Coast Design, Portland, Oregon

Cover illustration copyright © Carol Endres

Published in association with the literary agency of Alive Communications, Inc., 7680 Goddard Street, Suite 200, Colorado Springs, CO 80920

EVERYDAY ANGELS
Copyright © 2002 by Annette Smith
Published by Harvest House Publishers
Eugene, Oregon 97402

Library of Congress Cataloging-in-Publication Data
    Smith, Annette Gail, 1959-
      Everyday angels / Annette Smith.
        p. cm.
      ISBN 0-7369-0742-4
      1. Chistian life—Anecdotes. I. Title.

BV4517 .S625 2002
242—dc21   2001036774

Printed in the United States of America

05 06 07 08 09 10 / BP-MS / 10 9 8 7 6

For my brothers,
Dayne and Bruce

ACKNOWLEDGMENTS

Special thanks to—

My husband, Randy. When I'm feeling fearful and in over my head, Randy encourages me to step on out into deep waters. Most often I do. Knowing he'll be cheering from the shore makes all the difference.

My children, Russell and Rachel. Because they have been such wonderfully responsible and easy-to-rear kiddos, I've been free to pour large portions of energy into the crafting of books.

My parents, Louie and Marolyn Woodall. Their constant interest and never-ending words of encouragement lift my spirits and make me feel ready to take any challenge on.

My friends, Susan Duke, Rebecca Barlow Jordan, and Sheila Cook. They lent special prayers and support this time around.

My agent, Chip McGregor. I'm blessed to have such an adviser and guide.

The warm and friendly folks at Harvest House Publishers. I appreciate the wonderful job they do turning my ideas into lovely books.

To God be the glory.

Contents

PART FOUR: CLOCKING IN

REMEMBERING THE ANGELS

Before I was a year old, my mother began taking me to church with her every Sunday. There, for a solid hour (longer if it was Visiting Preacher Day—they always went over), she struggled to keep me quiet. I was a happy baby and rarely cried, but I did make lots of noise—babbling and jabbering nonsense the way all tots do. Though she gave me my blanket and my bottle and plied me with tiny bits of graham cracker, many Sundays my mother spent her entire worship hour worried about me disturbing the folks who sat in nearby pews.

One such morning, after the last "amen" had been said, a sweet-faced elderly woman approached and laid a kind hand on my mother's shoulder. "You *do* know, don't you, dear," she said with twinkling eyes, "that when little ones jabber and talk baby talk they're trying their hardest to tell us about the angels."

"The angels?" My mother thought she'd misheard.

"Yes, and of all the loveliness they got to see in heaven before they were born. The reason why we never get to hear about it"— she captured and kissed my chubby hand—"is that by the time babies are old enough to speak with words that we can understand, they've forgotten everything they saw. Isn't that a shame?"

My mother allowed that indeed it was.

"Honey," the old lady continued with a wink, "if I were you, I'd listen real close to this little one." She gave my chin a gentle tweak.

"From the way she's carrying on, I'd say she's got lots to say. Perhaps if you're lucky, you'll be able to make out a word or two before she forgets."

I've often wondered whether what that woman said is true. Do babies *really* get to see heaven before they are born? Try as I might, I can't remember a thing about angels—the ones that the old lady said I saw. Halos, wings, golden harps—I recall nothing like that. But gifted with a memory for detail and, as the old lady predicted, having lots to say, many other things I *do* recall—especially about folks who, despite being incredibly human and endearingly flawed, display angelic qualities like faith and hope, love and good humor. I call such folks *everyday angels.*

All of the stories in this book are about real people I've known and actual situations I've seen. However, to protect the innocence (or the guilt—see chapter 7!) of those I love, I've changed some of the names and identifying details. A few of the stories I've fancied up with fiction in hopes of spinning a more entertaining yarn.

It is my desire that you, dear reader, will enjoy these tales and that they will inspire you to look around with brand-new eyes. I encourage you to scout around for some everyday angels of your own. You'll find them—I'm sure of it. When you do, listen really hard—for everyday angels have great stories to tell.

WEDDED BLISS
PART ONE

CHAPTER ONE

SUMMER AFTERNOON NAP

Honestly—Jackie Lynn Bledsow did not think it a bit odd when on a Monday afternoon Aaron Lucky dialed her up to ask if she, by chance, had in her files a recipe for chocolate fudge bundt cake—the kind that makes its own glaze. Jackie Lynn was a high-school home economics teacher. Folks called her for recipes all the time. They also phoned for stain-removal hints, gardening tips, and for help with their sewing projects.

Why, certainly. She had exactly the recipe that Aaron needed. Should she recite it to him right now over the phone, or would he rather she write it down on a card and give it to him at Wednesday-night prayer meeting instead?

Prayer meeting would be fine.

And so she did.

The next Monday, he called again.

"Hello?"

"Jackie Lynn, this is Aaron Lucky. I was wondering if you could tell me what kind of batter you use to fry fish."

Sure she could. She was glad to help.

The next Monday it was biscuit batter that Aaron needed. Then egg custard, stewed tomatoes, peanut-butter pie, and tuna noodle casserole.

Tuna noodle casserole?

11

"Since when has Aaron Lucky become so interested in cooking?" smirked Jackie Lynn's sister, Tammy, who was visiting when he called.

Jackie Lynn shrugged. She didn't rightly know.

The truth? Since the death of his wife nine months ago. Since the loneliness, the silence in his house had become more than he could bear. Since Tammy's lovely sister, Jackie Lynn, had caught his eye.

What had happened was that Aaron Lucky, a thoughtful, methodical man, woke up one morning, threw back the covers, and decided that enough was enough. It was time—*past* time, actually—to set about finding a new wife. No disrespect to his beloved, now-departed Margaret, but after being blissfully wed for nearly 40 years, after learning to share everything from toothpaste to sofa space, he did not take well to living alone. He was tired of eating alone, drinking morning coffee alone, watching television alone.

Aaron *liked* being married. He *missed* having a wife.

On the morning that he decided to get married again, Aaron took out a yellow pad and made a list of all the single women who were members of his church. Below their names he listed each woman's most outstanding positive quality, and under that, what he thought to be her most troublesome trait.

> *Rosalie Bennett.*
> *Good cook.*
> *Six cats.*

Aaron was a dog man himself. He didn't see how that would work.

> *Hanna Foster.*
> *Nice figure* (really *nice*).
> *Blue hair.*

Aaron wasn't overconcerned about a woman's looks, but a man has to draw the line somewhere.

Jean Ennis.
Outgoing, vivacious, and friendly.
Five dead husbands.

Aaron got a bit queasy at the thought of becoming number six. Then he came to Jackie Lynn.

At 46, she was his junior by 12 years. Was that a problem? He thought not. She'd never been married, was a good cook, helpful, a little bit plump, and very pretty. She knew the Bible well and had proved to be a good conversationalist, yet didn't appear prone to incessant chatter like some women he had known. In his life, Aaron had run across a few women who talked so much that it set a body to wondering if perhaps they'd been given their baby shots with a Victrola needle.

Yes. Of those he had to choose from, Jackie Lynn was definitely the best of the lot. Aaron set out in hot pursuit. His repeated Monday recipe requests were just the warm-up. Following a carefully thought-out plan, on the second Wednesday of the month, he phoned Jackie Lynn to ask if she could possibly tell him how to remove blueberry stains from a polyester-blend shirt.

She could.

And on Thursday, he called to see if she could advise him on how best to keep mealworms from getting in his flour.

Finally, after three months of all this—"Jackie Lynn?"

"Yes?"

"Would you like to go out to dinner Friday night?"

She thought he would never ask.

Six weeks after their first real date, Aaron slipped an eye-popping, three-quarter-carat, emerald-cut diamond ring on Jackie Lynn's finger. Since she had always wanted to see Colorado, that's where they went on their honeymoon. The trip was—by Jackie Lynn's dreamy, pink-faced reports—simply bliss.

I met Mr. and Mrs. Lucky when I was working as a home-health nurse. They were, by then, 84 and 72 years young—and as cute as they could be. Tales of their late-in-life love story charmed me. The obvious affection they had for each other touched my heart. Their off-the-wall antics kept me entertained.

"Aaron and I slept in our clothes last night," Jackie Lynn confided to me one morning.

"Why?" I asked. Aaron wore overalls every day. All those buckles and straps! Heavy denim—that must have been terribly uncomfortable.

"Honey, didn't you hear that awful storm? Why, I was afraid that me and Aaron might get blown away. If that happened I didn't want us to be naked, so we slept in our clothes. I kept my purse around my arm all night too. You know I don't keep much money in there, but every time I go anywhere, someone asks to see my Social Security card. I think it's a good idea to always have it with me, don't you?"

I allowed that it was.

Aaron loved fried food. Jackie Lynn, on the advice of his doctor, didn't cook it for him. Ever. She boiled and baked all their meals instead.

This bothered Aaron a great deal. Fried chicken. Fried steak. Fried okra and squash. He missed them all. "I know she means well, but you can't tell me that folks don't need a little grease in their systems once in a while," he stated his point. "Long as it's *good* grease, you understand, like Crisco—not that cheap stuff—I don't see what it would hurt."

"Bad for your art-trees," Jackie Lynn would explain. "Doc Hardin said you're not supposed to have it."

So he didn't. Except when she wasn't around. Once a month, Jackie Lynn and the women at the church enjoyed what they called ladies' day out. They took the church bus into Dallas and stayed gone all day, having lunch, shopping, taking some kind of tour, maybe seeing a play.

Every day that Jackie Lynn was gone was Friday for Aaron. *Fry day.* He'd stand at the door and wave till she was out of sight, then shuffle to the kitchen and heat up the grease.

I know this because more than once I caught him at it. Both times, he bought my silence with a plate of tangy fried green tomatoes.

Though Jackie Lynn liked to go places with her friends, Aaron preferred not to leave the house without his wife. Which is why, the day I arrived for my regular visit and found Jackie Lynn cozied up in her recliner watching *General Hospital* with Aaron nowhere around, I was momentarily curious, then quickly concerned.

"Mrs. Lucky, how are you today?"

"I'm fine, save for a touch of arthritis."

"And Mr. Lucky?"

She looked around, not exactly confused, but rattled just the same. "Why, honey, I don't know where he is. Maybe he's in the bathroom."

"No, ma'am. I looked."

She turned suddenly pale. "Oh my." She rose from her chair. "I remember now. Aaron and I were out in the yard picking pecans up off the ground. He fell down and I couldn't get him up. I came in to call for help, but then I saw that my story—you know how I love *All My Children*—was on and…oh goodness, that was more than two hours ago! He's been out there all this time."

We rushed out the back door. When I saw him lying out flat, I feared he was dead.

"Mr. Lucky!"

"Aaron!"

"Are you all right?"

"Should I call 9-1-1?"

"I'm not sure. Let me check him and see." I knelt in the grass beside him. "Mr. Lucky? Mr. Lucky?" I placed my hand on his shoulder and gave him a gentle shake. *Look, listen, and feel for breathing.* I recited the CPR steps in my mind.

Suddenly Mr. Lucky opened his eyes, stretched, and let out a big wheezy yawn. "Hi, girls. Can you help me to my feet? I believe I've had all of the nap I need."

He was fine.

Once she'd dried her eyes, Jackie Lynn was so relieved that she decided to make him a southern-fried steak-and-potato dinner that night. "Honey, do you think it will hurt him?" she asked me. "He loves it so."

"Not one bit," I assured her. "Mrs. Lucky, as long as you use *good* grease, I don't believe it will hurt him one bit."

> *I will be your God throughout your lifetime—*
> *until your hair is white with age.*
> *I made you, and I will care for you.*
> *I will carry you along and save you.*
> ISAIAH 46:4 (NLT)

CHAPTER TWO

SLEEPING TRIPLE
IN A DOUBLE BED

Jack Malone passed his last final exam on Tuesday, graduated from a Christian college on Friday, and in a moving double-ring ceremony, married his sweetheart, Katie McCord, on Sunday afternoon.

While the just-married couple nibbled cake and sipped fruit punch, Katie's four younger brothers and Jack's two nearly grown sisters filled the cab of Jack's pickup truck with balloons. (*Balloons*, it should be noted. At the rehearsal dinner the night before the wedding, Katie's historically true-to-her-word mother had gotten in their faces and informed the whole innocent-acting bunch of them that she would *personally* dismember them *all* should she find out that they had used even *one* of a certain *other* inflatable item to decorate the newlyweds' car.) The rowdy troop scrawled risqué shoe-polish sayings on the back window, sprayed shaving cream on all the door handles, and tied tin cans and old tennis shoes to the bumper of the U-Haul trailer that was already loaded and hitched to the rear of Jack's truck.

Jack eased his truck from under the awning of the church, and the front of the trailer scraped bottom as the new couple pulled out onto the street. Both their mothers cried, both their fathers pretended not to want to, and all six brothers and sisters sprinted their way back to the reception room, hoping for leftover wedding cake.

As they neared the edge of town, 22-year-old Jack, smart and serious, was the first one to speak. Drawing his wife of only two hours close, he spoke. "Katie, I'm the luckiest guy in the world. Today feels like the first day of my life. Really. Finishing school, getting married to you, starting my new job…"

She snuggled in so close that Jack could smell the roses in her going-away corsage. He stroked her hair, squeezed her shoulder, and indulged in only the quickest of glances down the front of her blouse. "How is it going to feel to be a youth minister's wife?"

"It feels just right."

"You ready for this?"

"I'm ready."

He kissed the top of her head.

Today, 22 years, 44 weeks of summer camp, and 353 hot-dog suppers later, Katie can say that it still feels just right to be a youth minister's wife. She loves kids—even the blue-haired, body-pierced ones of late—and has been there beside Jack since day one. So valued is her work with the teens, folks who know them well often comment that the churches where she and Jack serve get great two-for-the-price-of-one deals.

Church youth work has changed in the years since Jack and Katie started at their first little congregation more than two decades ago. Kids have changed. Families have changed. Even churches have changed.

Used to be that kids had little else to do besides go to school and take part in youth-group activities. Now, young people are involved in all kinds of time-consuming activities: sports, sports, and more sports, drama, scouts, and music lessons—not to mention part-time jobs. Every year there is more competition for kids' time and more to distract them from church involvement.

When Katie and Jack first started working with teens, most kids came from intact families. These days more than a quarter of their charges live in single-parent homes; another quarter are parented by complicated setups involving sometimes multiple sets of step-moms and stepdads.

Drugs, alcohol, and sexual temptations have been present in the lives of youth forever. But it is only in recent years that teens' involvement in them has become so common an occurrence as to not shock even the most staid-looking church lady sitting on a pew.

Then again, some characteristics of teenagers have not changed one bit.

Kids *still* love amusements parks. Just as in years past, Jack knows to count on every kid who has *ever* been to church to show up in the parking lot right on time for an amusement park trip—and to bring along his three best friends. *And* Jack knows to count on that same kind of kid (and his three best friends) to always be the ones late to meet back on the bus.

Though just as in days past, a good percentage of teens routinely skip Sunday school to hang out in their cars, and pass notes during worship time, and fall asleep during the sermon, Jack and Katie have learned that without fail the entire irreverent bunch of them can be depended upon to show up in great numbers to paint a widow woman's porch for free. They will be there every time, and it won't matter that the temperature outside is 103 in the shade.

Kids *still* crave the attention and affection of caring adults. Most afternoons, a handful of teens show up at Katie and Jack's house after school. They prop themselves up on bar stools in the kitchen, munch on cookies, and talk to Katie about what's going on at school and at home. Hungry-for-God teenagers, now as then, greedily claim the love of Jesus with a depth of transparent repentance and brokenhearted confession that never ceases to take Katie and Jack's breath.

It is why they still do what they do.

I met Katie and Jack more than a dozen years ago, when Randy and I were members at the church where they were serving. The four of us had children the same ages, had been married about the same number of years, and enjoyed lots of common interests. Many Saturday afternoons the guys watched sports while Katie and I worked on crafts or scouted junk stores hoping to discover some rare and hidden antique. We had great times together, and though we haven't lived in the same town for years now, our families keep in touch and manage to visit at least once a year.

Back then, Randy and I both regularly helped Jack and Katie with youth activities. We liked serving together, and it was only because of a conflict with Randy's work schedule that one March I ended up helping chaperone the teens' first annual ski trip without him.

Randy wasn't the only person with scheduling conflicts. What with choir contests, travels to see grandparents, and mandatory holiday visits with noncustodial parents, orchestrating a five-day ski trip to a six-hours-away resort the week after Christmas proved to be more of a challenge than Jack planned for. While the majority of the kids could leave on the originally scheduled day, some of them would need to come a day or more late. Unwilling for any kid who wanted to go to be left out, Jack made arrangements to meet parents halfway for odd arrivals and departures. There were to be so many such meetings that, when I glimpsed Jack's complicated list of who was to be picked up or delivered where and when, I got a headache.

I still had that headache a day later when Katie and I pulled into the parking lot of the hotel where we would stay the night in preparation for the early-morning meeting and pickup of three late-to-arrive teens. Jack would arrive the next morning, coming in from the other direction after meeting up with a kid who'd been visiting his grandma. We would all travel together back to the resort.

By tomorrow afternoon, everyone should have either arrived on their own or been collected by an adult sponsor. I was looking forward to watching the teens enjoy the slopes as a group.

Katie and I didn't arrive at the hotel until well after ten. By the time we got checked in, both of us were so exhausted that we went straight to bed. As we looked ahead to the next four nights we'd spend sleeping on bunk beds in a drafty group dorm—kept company by no less than 40 giggling teenage girls and six snoring adult women sponsors—the prospect of one night in a real bed was too delicious to resist.

"Good night," I told Katie.

"Good night."

"Mmm, what time's Jack supposed to be here?" Drowsy, I couldn't remember what time we needed to get up.

"Eight," Katie answered.

"We can sleep till seven?"

"Seven-thirty."

"Wonderful."

" 'Night."

Her words are the last sound I remember hearing.

Until a quarter of three.

Katie and I sat straight up, dazed and confused, awakened by someone pounding on the hotel room door. "Who could that be?" I rubbed my eyes.

"I dunno." Katie groped for her glasses.

"Where's the phone? I'm calling Security."

"Is the safety bolt locked?"

Then Jack's voice. "Katie. Open up. It's me, Jack."

Jack?

I stayed in bed while Katie opened up the door. "What are you doing, Jack? It's the middle of the night! You scared us to death! What's wrong? Has there been an emergency?"

Jack stood slump-shouldered, stomping and shivering in the doorway. "No, no. No emergency. Just a big mix-up. I ended up heading back here instead of picking up the kid. The van broke down but I got it fixed. Then the kid didn't show up when he was supposed to. It's a long story." Jack looked past Katie to see me still hunched under the covers of the one bed in the room. "I was going to get a room, but the hotel's booked. I'm sorry I woke you up but I wanted you to know I was here in case you needed me. Go back to bed. I'm just going to sit the rest of the night out in the van. I'll see you in the morning."

"Jack," Katie protested, "it's freezing out there!"

"I'll be fine. Don't worry."

"Ja-ack," Katie protested.

I threw back the covers. "Come on, Jack, you are *not* sleeping in the van. Get in this room right now." It occurs to me now that the splendid sight of me in red-flannel footed pajamas and under-the-eye-mascara *could* in theory have incited lust in his heart. No matter. Brazen woman that I am, I flipped on the bedside lamp with a wanton flourish. "Look, we have to be on the road in less than five hours. You need sleep. We need sleep. We are all three exhausted, and it is too cold for you to sleep in the van. Now come on in and close the door. There's plenty of room for you to sleep with us."

(I've been told by my husband that I get a *teensy* bit bossy when I'm overtired. Surely he jests.)

"But there's just one bed."

Can't say the man's not observant.

"I guess I *could* stretch out here on the floor." Jack looked longingly at the big king-sized bed.

"Nonsense," I told him. "I'll sleep on this side. Katie can sleep in the middle, and you can sleep on the other side of her."

"I don't know about this," he hedged.

Katie was grumpy by now. "Oh, Jack, just hush up and get in bed. We're all too tired for a big discussion. Get some sleep."

Jack did as he was told. Cold and weary, he climbed fully clothed under the covers next to Katie. Within minutes we were all sound asleep.

The next morning all three of us were in a better mood. As we put on our shoes and our jackets, prepared to head out, I sneaked a wink at Katie. "You know, Jack, we did what we had to do last night, but I've heard you tell the kids over and over that we should all avoid even the appearance of evil. Come Sunday, I'm thinking that you and I should go down to the front of the church and let everyone in on our little incident."

"Our *incident?*" I watched as every bit of color drained from Jack's face.

"Oh, I know that some people won't understand," I continued with feigned nonchalance. "I expect we'll have to go before the board and, sure, there'll be those who won't believe us when we tell them that *nothing happened...*"

Jack broke out in a sweat. I saw it on his brow.

"...but we won't worry about them, will we, Jack?" I still managed to maintain a straight face, but my lips began to twitch.

"Uh...I'm not so sure...uh...that we need to...uh..."

"What are you saying, Jack?" Katie, standing behind him, struggled not to laugh.

"Maybe it would be best if we...I mean...perhaps we should..." He stuttered and stumbled all over the place. Katie let loose a snort.

Finally I let him out of his misery. "Jack, I'm kidding!"

He was not. "I think it would be better if we kept this to ourselves. There is no need for anyone else to know that we...I mean, not that we..."

Katie was doubled over by then.

"Don't you agree?" he asked of his wife.

"Sure, Jack. I promise not to tell *anyone* that you and Annette slept together. In a hotel. On a *church* trip. I won't tell the elders.

I won't tell the deacons. I won't even tell the youth council. On my honor."

Poor Jack. He is one of the most morally upright men I have ever met. He loves his wife, loves his kids. Not once, do I believe, has my friend Jack set one little toe over the line of marital fidelity. Bless his heart. I'm afraid that our little hotel-room "incident" nearly did him in. Even now, when the four of us get together and someone mentions it, he starts to squirm.

So of course, every time that the four of us get together, Katie and I make absolutely sure that it *does* come up!

When I called Katie to ask what she thought about me telling this story, I assured her, "I'll change your names and enough of the details that no one will guess that it's you and Jack I'm writing about."

She didn't hesitate. "Go for it, Annette."

And so I did.

(Don't worry, Jack. Your secret is safe with me!)

> *Dear friend, I pray…that all may go well with you,*
> *even as your soul is getting along well.*
> 3 JOHN 2

CHAPTER THREE

THANKS WHERE THANKS IS DUE

Annie's husband, Ed, good-naturedly lays equal blame for the embarrassing situation both on his wife and the Pentecostals at the First Church of the Lamb. Annie disagrees, claiming to this day that Ed and the boys brought it upon themselves—and that the Pentecostals were just doing what Pentecostals do. Besides, since all eyes were supposed to be closed—*in prayer,* she pointedly reminds him—how can he be 100-percent sure that that it was the Pentecostals anyway?

"Could just as easily have been the Zion's Rest Baptists, or even the Birch Street Methodists," Annie maintains.

Ed scoffs and shakes his head. "Honey, no offense intended, but it *was* the Pentecostals."

Like he's some religious *expert.*

The church denomination to which Annie and Ed belong is the same conservative one in which they both grew up. Though it's not perfect, there are lots of reasons why it's the place where they've decided to rear their four boys—even though many of their friends have transferred their memberships to one of the bigger, hipper churches that are attracting so many of the young families in their town. The church of their childhood is a place full of good, helpful people who believe that the Bible is God's Word and that things should be done in the way that He says.

Because they've been going there for so long, when they and their four stairstepped, crew-cut sons show up for worship—when they slide themselves into their regular pew—they do so knowing exactly what to expect. Once things get going, there'll be three hymns and a prayer, one more hymn, and a 30-minute sermon. The sermon will be followed by an invitation hymn, then announcements, one more hymn. A brief dismissal prayer will wrap things up.

Being that the church's starting time is 30 minutes earlier than any of the rest in town, unless they tarry and talk, those worshipers who choose to eat out find themselves first in line at the downtown cafeteria. Smart, don't you agree? By the time the rest of the Sunday crowd arrives, members of Ed and Annie's church are wiping their mouths, pushing back their chairs, and heading home to newspapers and naps.

Just so you know, they are a restrained group—Annie and Ed's church family. They're traditional in their approach to worship, and you won't find any among them clapping, shouting, or lifting their hands. (Though occasionally in response to certain rousing hymns from the 1940s, some members can be observed stealthily tapping their feet.) Like their fellow worshipers, Annie and Ed and the boys sit in their pews unless they're told to stand. They sing the hymns that are printed in the books, and they silently bow their heads when it is time to pray.

Ed, by nature a calm and contented man, sees no reason why things should be done any other way. He was married in that church, and he plans to be buried in the cemetery behind it. It was good enough for his mama and daddy, and it most certainly is good enough for him and his too.

Most of the time Annie is just as happy with their chosen congregation as is her husband. After all, he doesn't force her to go there or anything like that. She and Ed together made the prayerful choice about which church body their family would belong to.

Like Ed, Annie finds comfort in doing things the same way every time and in knowing exactly what's coming next.

Most of the time.

Like Ed, Annie appreciates the orderliness of it all.

Most of the time.

Like Ed, Annie thinks that their church is the best place for their family.

Most of the time.

Yet, when she's struck by one of her periodic bouts of discontent, Annie finds herself longing for a little lift, for a wee bit more emotion, for a few of the inspiring-sounding frills that some of her across-town churchgoing friends describe. She wonders, sometimes, whether she and her family are missing out by confining their worship to such a traditional style.

"Drama? In church? How does that work?" she asks her friend Linda.

"You're right, that is a beautiful song," she agrees with her neighbor Chris, after hearing a tape of the modern cantata that Chris's church choir is putting on.

"Everyone prayed with their faces to the floor?" She's never seen anything like that done.

That mood came upon her, yet again, one Sunday in the fall. Settled into her pew between Ed and the boys, instead of feeling comfortable and at home, Annie found in her heart a seed of criticism and discontent, bound and determined to sprout and grow. The day's designated song leader, Annie noticed, was off key. The publicly prayed prayers were long and rambling. (Did God not already know which hospital each of the sick were in?) The preacher, who she loves and admires, delivered a yawner of a sermon if she had ever heard one.

"So what are you saying?" asks Ed as they stretch out together for a Sunday-afternoon nap. "Are you wanting to change churches?" They've had this talk before. He also knows what it is she'll say.

"No. Of course not. I love our church. I believe in what it stands for. There are good people there. I don't want to leave. It's just that sometimes I feel like I need something more."

"Like what?"

"I don't know—maybe I just ought to read a book or something."

"I betcha that will help." He turns over and is soon asleep.

Later in the week, Annie reads in the newspaper of an event she thinks might give her spiritual life just the boost that it needs. It would be good for the whole family, and they wouldn't have to miss a single service at their home church.

"Thanksgiving service?" repeats Ed. "I didn't know we were doing any kind of special service. I don't remember us ever doing one before."

"Not us. The community. They're having it at Grace Street Bible Church because it has the biggest building."

"And you want us to go."

"It would mean a lot." She turns her head to the side in a way that he always finds cute. "I think it would do us all some good. Besides, it wouldn't hurt the boys to see that not everyone worships the same way that we do."

Ed resigns himself to going, even though he figures there will probably be *drums*.

Come Thursday night, Annie and her cajoled-into-coming-along family sit stiff and overdressed, like soldiers, just inside the back wall of a church not their own (a church with *theater seats* instead of pews, with an *overhead projector* instead of songbooks, for heaven sakes!). The five of them are welcome, if uncomfortable and unsure, guests at this service, sponsored by the County Alliance of Christian Churches—an organization to which, it should be noted, their church does not belong.

Annie and Ed and the boys are not the only visitors. The whole citizenry of the town has been invited, via full-color newspaper ads and photocopied flyers hung on the front door of every business in town. The place is so packed that obviously much of the town has taken the church up on its invitation.

The intent of organizers of this community-wide event was, from the beginning, to foster unity among the different churches, to inspire members of various denominations to see themselves as one body. Things have not exactly worked out that way. Perhaps, in their hearts, the folk who have arrived this night do indeed *feel* unified, but from the looks of the already filled rows of seats, friendly, though fierce, competition has broken out. Every church represented is hoping to have a bigger contingency than any of the others. As folks drift in, squinty-eyed from the contrast of darkness to light, they are met by members of their home churches.

"Jack, Sue, we're all over here."

"Scoot down, here come four more!"

"Looks like we've got the biggest group."

"I don't know. Faith Presbyterian is closing in. How much longer until time to start?"

Folks roam the aisles, looking for stray members, finding them, and instigating moves so as to increase their denominational ranks.

But Annie, Ed and the boys sit in a row by themselves. Ed, who loves Annie very much, can't even begin to understand why they are here. He fidgets in his seat and sneaks glances at his watch when he thinks she's not looking.

The boys are pouting. All four of them sit with their arms folded across their chests. This is weird. They don't like it. This place is not the same as their church. And it's not even Wednesday night.

Annie, despite her best efforts, feels as out of place as does the rest of her family. Ed was right, she thinks. They should not have come. After all of her big talk, she doesn't want to be here either. Perhaps it wouldn't be too rude to just slip out the back door. But it's too late. The service begins.

First a welcome is given. A warm one at that.

Annie feels Ed and the boys relax. The preacher at their church always gives a welcome too.

Next comes a song.

"Amazing Grace." One that they know. Then "We Gather Together." They know that one too. Ed and the boys love to sing.

Annie thinks that maybe, after all, it *is* good that they've come.

Finally, a prayer—and as prayers go, one of pretty standard stuff. First there is praise, then pleas for the sick, requests for guidance, and for forgiveness of sins. Ed and Annie and the boys bow along with the rest, concentrating on the prayer leader's words.

"...and God, we thank you for this special day..." he prays.

"*Yes, Lord,*" responds someone in a pew near the front right of the sanctuary.

The interruption startles the boys. They are used to silence when someone prays. They raise their heads, but Annie motions for them to bow. They know better than to disrespect a prayer.

"...for all of the bounty that you have blessed us with."

"*Yes-s-s-s-s Lord.*" This time several voices in unison say the affirming words.

Annie opens her eyes to see Ed squeezing his shut—and putting his hand to his mouth.

"*Yes-s-s-s-s-s-s-s-s! Yes-s-s-s-s-s-s-s-s Lord!*" Forty voices at least. To folks unaccustomed to such, the collective effect is unfortunately that of a bunch of hissing snakes.

Annie can take no more. She steals a glance at Ed. He is silent, seemingly expressionless—but he's doubled over in his seat. All four boys look like they may blow at any minute. As soon as the last "amen" is said, Annie catches the eye of each of them. On a silent count of three, the five of them rise, exit their seats, and politely bolt for the door.

Six Novembers have passed since that night. Six community-wide Thanksgiving services. Six appearances of Ed and Annie and their four boys.

They never miss.

It was to Annie's surprise that Ed had insisted they go back the next year. And the year after that. About the same time, it was at Ed's suggestion that the family began their annual attendance at the city-wide Independence Day prayer services and Easter sunrises out at the lake.

Not to worry. They still belong to the same conservative, traditional church. It is where they feel most at home. But Ed now says that he sees a lot of good coming out of a variety of folks— imperfect though they may be—coming together to praise a perfect God.

As for Annie, she is thrilled. Her need for a spiritual shot in the arm is fulfilled by these means. And today, when Annie looks back, do you wonder who it is she thanks?

Why, the Pentecostals—of course!

Yes Lord, indeed!

> *Yes, LORD,*
> *walking in the way of your laws, we wait for you;*
> *your name and renown are the desire of our hearts.*
> ISAIAH 26:8

CHAPTER FOUR

RUBY AND LAW

They made quite a pair.

Law was a tall, handsome, and strong young man of mixed Irish heritage. Born into a southern household that was rich in sons but poor in cash, Law learned at a young age to shrink from neither the hardest of work nor the fiercest of fights. By the time he was a grown-up man of 21, Law excelled at both.

Ruby was a halfway orphan from the first day of life; her 17-year-old mother had died giving birth to her. Because her sad young father was unable to take care of a baby by himself, Ruby's grandmother took her in. She lived with her until she was 13. That year, her grandmother died too, and Ruby went to live, for the first time in her life, with her daddy, her stepmother, and a noisy batch of half brothers and sisters.

It was in a tiny Texas town that teenagers Law and Ruby met and fell in love. He liked looking into Ruby's eyes and thought it was cute the way her left one turned in just a bit. Ruby liked Law's height and strength. She was impressed by the way he always appeared to know just exactly what it was he wanted to do.

Which was to marry her.

As soon as possible.

At first, both of their families approved of the union. Wedding plans were made, and Ruby and Law thrilled at the prospect of being together. Then suddenly, Ruby's daddy changed his mind.

He told Ruby there was no way he would let her marry Law. The couple was bitterly disappointed but held out hope that Ruby's daddy would change his mind.

When weeks went by and his mind stayed set, Law got tired of waiting and concocted a plan of his own. It was a simple plan, really. On a sunny afternoon, he picked up Ruby's best girlfriend in his Model-T Ford. Together, they drove up close to where Ruby lived but parked to the side of the railroad track, out of sight of her house. Law waited in the car while Ruby's girlfriend got out to fetch his bride-to-be.

Once inside, barely out of her stepmother's earshot, Ruby's girlfriend whispered the plan, "You've got to hurry. Law's waiting for you at the end of the lane. He's come for you."

"You mean…" Ruby's eyes got big. So unexpected was this turn of events that she could barely breathe, much less collect her thoughts enough to know what to do next.

"Come on," urged her friend. "Tell your stepmother that you're going for a walk with me. Tell her you'll be back in time to help her fix supper."

The lies came easily. Her stepmother did not suspect a thing. When the girls got to Law's car, he opened the door for them. "Ruby," he said, patting the seat beside him, "let's go get ourselves hitched."

"Now? Are you sure?"

"Sure as I can be."

After letting Ruby's girlfriend out at her house, Law drove straight to the preacher's house. They got out and, hand in hand, mounted the steps leading to the front door.

Law knocked.

They waited.

Ruby could not stop her trembling—she was getting *married! Today! Right now! This could not be!* She had on an old, faded, checked school dress. She was wearing heavy black stockings. And they had holes in them!

Law was steady and sure.

Together they waited until the preacher came and let them in. He was a kind man, his wife a plump and friendly woman. Accustomed to interruptions such as this, they invited Law and Ruby right in, told them to have a seat and to make themselves at home while she put on her better shoes and while he got his glasses and his Bible.

Obediently, Ruby and Law sat side by side on the preacher's firm couch, not touching, neither saying a word, and waited for what felt like a very long time. Once Ruby coughed. Twice Law looked at his watch. At last, the preacher came back into the room and told them both to stand. Oddly, he directed them to a spot on the floor in front of a wide, full-length mirror. It was there, looking past the preacher and into the reflections of their own eyes, that Ruby and Law took their vows.

"Looking yourself in the eye while you say such serious words sure makes you think about what it is you're doing," Ruby later told her best friend.

By that night, Ruby's daddy had heard the news. Though angry and hurt, he knew that there was nothing that he could do. Eventually he accepted his daughter's marriage, but the morning after he'd heard he was so shook that he got up and walked all the way to town with his overalls on backwards.

Although Ruby hoped to have children right off, she and Law had been married for several years before a daughter, Joy, came along. She, a dark-haired beauty, was followed two years later by a son they named Louie.

The early years of their marriage were difficult ones. The country's economy, held in the vise grip of the Great Depression, struggled and staggered. Work was scarce and money tight. Ruby and Law made do picking cotton, milking a cow, and keeping chickens and a garden, but during those years they both grew lean.

Then times got better for the whole country—and for Law and Ruby too.

Joy and Louie grew up and made families of their own. By then, Law and Ruby owned a patch of land and a house—which Law built with his own hands—free and clear. In the safety deposit box at the bank were paid-up life insurance policies, and a savings account held enough of a nest egg that the couple felt as secure as any member of their generation ever would.

Law and Ruby still kept their garden, but Law no longer had to work as a carpenter every day. Gifted at coaxing life from the ground, the hours Law and Ruby spent tilling the earth were so well rewarded that, year after year, even after supplying their friends, family, and neighbors with food for their tables, there was ample produce left to sell at the farmers' market.

It was during the second half of their married life that Law and Ruby could finally relax and have some fun. Law liked to fish. Often on his way out the door to the pond, he teased Ruby that he was going to his office.

Both of them loved to play dominoes, but best of all they liked to sing. Though neither of them could play a note, at an auction they bought a used upright piano so they could host Saturday-night gospel singings at their house. Many summer nights, if the wind was just right, the melded soprano, alto, tenor, and bass voices of up to 40 of their neighbors and friends could be heard nearly a quarter mile up the road.

Law liked "The Old Rugged Cross."

Ruby loved "In the Sweet By and By."

Those were some very good years.

Early in his 70s, on a cold November night, Law ate a bowl of cornflakes, crawled under one of Ruby's handmade quilts, and went to sleep. He never woke up. Just like that, Law was gone.

His passing was hard on his children and his grandchildren, but especially difficult for Ruby to bear. For months, she would look out into the pasture, past the grove of pecan trees, and think she saw him standing there, checking on the cattle like he'd always done. Though she didn't think she could go on without him, somehow, buoyed by the love of family, neighbors, and friends, like widows prior and hence, she did.

Ruby was my grandmother. We buried her this morning. She was 92 and had been sick for a very long time. After a months-long vigil at her bedside, my dad, Louie, and my Aunt Joy elected to forgo a traditional funeral in favor of an informal memorial service at the graveside. The rest of the family agreed. It was not to be a time of mourning, but a celebration of her life, an acknowledgment of her final homegoing.

When the hour of the service came, right according to plan, my brothers, Dayne and Bruce, spoke a few prepared words. My sister-in-law Dale and I read from the book of Psalms. We sang her favorite hymn. My cousin Robert said a prayer.

All who cared to were given the opportunity to stand and speak, and many did. They talked about Ruby and of what they recalled the best. Their remembrances were of simple things, of shared cotton-field confidences, of fried okra and sweet berry cobblers, of domino games and homemade ice cream.

Finally the last person to speak sat back down, and the great pause that occurs whenever such a service draws to a close settled around us. It was not until then that, despite our best intentions, many of us felt our throats become tight and our eyes fill with tears.

This was it.

All of it.

Never again would we, this group of family and friends, gather at Ruby's feet.

The service was over, but we hated to leave.

It was at that still moment, during that sad pause, that several small children, weary of sitting still and staying quiet, suddenly and simultaneously escaped from their mothers' and daddies' arms and ran out into the graveyard. No one went after them. Instead, huddled under my grandmother's funeral tent, we mourners watched as in the distance, like freed butterflies, the children ran and played, skipped, twirled, and danced in the sunshine. Their fresh faces and bright clothing shone in brilliant contrast to the dull gray stones.

And it was in the watching of those children that we, Ruby's descendants, were reminded of what we already knew.

Life goes on.

> *To every thing there is a season,*
> *and a time to every purpose under the heaven:*
> *A time to be born, and a time to die.*
> ECCLESIASTES 3:1,2 (KJV)

CHAPTER FIVE

ONE COOL COUPLE

Every fall, as predictable as pumpkins on porches, from the year of his birth until the day he started kindergarten, T.L. Mosby set up a howl on the first day of school. He watched his brothers and sisters board the bus and couldn't believe that they would leave him behind. Through indignant hot tears:

"Where are they going?"

"Why can't I go too?"

"How old do you have to be?"

"Well, when will *I* be that old?"

T.L., you see, simply *hated* to be alone. Couldn't stand it. Craving attention and talk, during his preschool years he nearly drove his poor mother crazy. Unlike other youngsters, who could entertain themselves with books and toys or spend sunny afternoons romping outside, T.L. didn't like to play by himself, eat by himself, or even sleep by himself.

Share a bed with his brothers?

Great! He'd like that.

Sit wedged into the middle of the backseat on a long car trip?

No problem. The more the merrier.

As long as there were other kids around he was happy.

T.L.'s gregarious nature didn't change as he got older. In high school he played three sports while serving as an officer for both the bridge club and the Christian athletes club. Friday nights he was always on a date or at a classmate's house. Saturdays he spent behind the counter at Tom's Auto Parts.

No one was surprised when T.L. got married. Only days out of high school, he marched straight down the aisle, arm in arm with his girlfriend of two years, Opal Reynolds, thrilled with the knowledge he would never be alone again. Someone to eat with? Someone to sleep with? T.L. wondered why *everyone* didn't get married at 18.

T.L. got off work at three each day. Soon as he clocked out, he raced straight home to see what Opal was doing. Washing dishes? He'd help dry. Working in the flower beds? He'd pull weeds. T.L. would do anything to be by Opal's side. A wife wise beyond her years, Opal tolerated her new husband's constant desire for company, with the only stipulation being that he please let her go into the bathroom by herself. Anywhere else he was welcome—the beauty shop, the market, even the church women's evening sewing circle, long as he stayed in the back corner and read his book.

Opal's unconditional acceptance of T.L. made it all the harder on him when, after 23 years of marriage, she died in her sleep.

T.L. meant no disrespect to his dear Opal, but the town gossips weren't far off when they snidely remarked that, since T.L. remarried so fast, he must have started courting at Opal's funeral.

Rosie, T.L.'s wife number two, like Opal, was what people refer to as a *good woman*. She was a good cook, a good housekeeper, a good churchgoer. What more could any man want? Compassionate and kind, Rosie treated T.L. just fine. Those who knew Opal believed that up in heaven she approved of the match. She of all people would have understood how it nearly killed T.L. to be by himself.

So what if it was only three weeks since her death?

T.L. took good care of both his wives. He never forgot their birthdays or anniversaries. He noticed when they put a permanent wave in their hair and always told them they looked nice when they got ready for church. When they wanted new carpet for the den, he let them pick it out. When they asked him to help paint the porch, he was down on his knees. So grateful was T.L. to have company, he thought whatever either wife did was just right.

T.L. and Rosie had been married eight years when she suddenly started acting strange. An intelligent woman, overnight his wife couldn't remember the simplest of things. After a lifetime possessed of an even temper, she began to cry at the drop of a hat. T.L. was afraid there was something badly wrong.

"Dear, it's The Change," her doctor explained in a gentle voice. "Nothing to worry about. We'll fix you right up." Aside to T.L.— who of course had come along—"Better get you a warm jacket, Mr. Mosby. Trust me. You're going to need it."

The doctor was right. A month or so later, a suddenly agitated Rosie asked, "T.L., are you hot?"

"No, honey. I'm fine. Why? Are you?" This did not seem to be a big deal. Rosie was a large woman, he a thin man. She tended to stay a bit warmer than him.

"I'm burning up. Is the air conditioner working?"

"I think so, but I'll check." He got up and looked. Sixty-eight degrees. "Looks to be working fine, sug'. How about some lemonade?"

"No. No lemonade, but could you turn the thermostat thing down a notch? I'm sweating a river." Red-faced Rosie popped a hormone pill, fanned herself, and mopped at her brow, none of which helped her feel cool.

T.L. felt sorry for his wife. He tried everything he knew to make her feel better, but over the next few weeks the hot flashes got worse. She was miserable. So was he. Rosie was hot when she worked, hot when she rested, hot when she sat on the pew at church.

Rosie was especially hot when she tried to go to sleep at night.

When the month of Rosie's birthday rolled around, T.L. came up with a plan. He would surprise her with a small window air conditioner for their bedroom—to go with the electric blanket on his side of the bed. That way she could feel cold air blowing right on her. He planned how to buy it without her finding out.

At Sears, while Rosie shopped for a Crock-Pot and some shoes, T.L. sidled over to the air conditioners. "Back in a second, honey. I need a new wrench." This shouldn't take long. He could pick out the air conditioner, pay for it, and arrange for delivery all before Rosie decided on sandals or pumps.

"May I help you?" The young sales clerk had a pencil behind his ear and a well-stocked plastic protector in his shirt pocket. "Air conditioner? Certainly. Right over here. We have several models to choose from, each with a different BTU rating."

"BTU?" T.L. didn't know what that was.

"British Thermal Unit." The young man paused to push his glasses up on his nose. "I'd be happy to explain the formula to you, but in layman's terms, the BTU tells how well a particular unit will cool. For instance, this particular model has only 1,200 BTU s. That one there has 45,000."

"Will it cool a 12-by-14-foot room?" T.L. asked.

"Sir, that depends. If you're putting it into use in combination with additional cooling systems, you'll want to be sure that your number of BTU s is appropriate for the amount of square footage you're trying to cool. However, if you don't go with a high enough BTU you won't get the most from your energy dollar."

T.L. glanced over his shoulder to see if Rosie was coming.

"Another way of looking at BTUs is…"

T.L. interrupted. Placing his hand on the young salesman's shoulder, he pointed to an area across the store. "Son, you see that woman over there?"

"Yes, sir."

"The one looking for queen-size panty hose?"

"Uh, yes…"

"Son, my sweet wife's got a B-U-T round as a T-U-B. It's hot and she wants it cool. I am not an educated man. I don't know anything about BTUs, but can you just sell me an air conditioner before she gets back over here?"

"Oh yes, sir. Absolutely, sir. This model right here should do a good job of cooling your wife's bot—I mean it will make your wife...uh, sir, will this be cash or Sears charge?"

God has brought me laughter,
and everyone who hears about this will laugh with me.
GENESIS 21:6

CHAPTER SIX

WITH A BOW ON TOP

Frank and Dee Dee Mize's son Chip moved himself and all his stuff back home after graduating from college in May. The couple were parents of four boys, and Chip's return marked the first time in five years that his empty-nester mom and dad had one of their children living under their roof.

The Mizes were a close family, and when Dee Dee and Frank's boys first began leaving home, they took it hard. On the morning that they delivered their oldest son, Marc, to an across-the-state university, the two of them hung around on campus for two days before finally waving their goodbyes. Leaving their oldest baby there just tore Dee Dee and Frank up inside. So brokenhearted were they at the realization that Marc would no longer be at home with the rest of the family, neither of them said a word during the entire three-hour drive home.

When Marc's next younger brother graduated and went to college, his departure was less devastating. Once they had him settled into his dorm, Frank and Dee Dee stayed for only one day and one night before heading home. Sure, there were tears, but not so many of them. And yes, there was silence in the car, but not the whole trip.

When son number three was left at his university, Dee Dee and Frank sniffled a bit, dabbed at their eyes, but left in time to get home before dark.

As for Chip's leaving? Pros by now, Frank and Dee Dee took him to school, unloaded his stuff, kissed him goodbye, and were on their way home in less than three hours.

For as one by one the number of kids at home decreased, Dee Dee and Frank came to the belief that having all of their offspring grown and out of the house would actually be a wonderful thing. And it was! They had married young, started their family right off, and hence had never had much time to focus on each other. Once the kids were gone, they made up for lost time, enjoying quiet dinners, nights out together, and weekend travel—not to mention plenty of hot water, an open phone line, and space in the garage to park both their cars.

Truth be told, they *loved* having their boys grown and gone.

Yet when Chip needed a place to stay, they welcomed him with open arms. After all, his return-to-the-nest housing arrangement was only temporary, planned to last a couple of months—three, tops. After five years of college, Chip, the youngest and the least motivated of their four, finally boasted a degree in history and a fall contract to teach.

The summer that Chip lived at home things went okay. Really they did. He tried to be polite. His parents tried to be polite. He helped out around the house. Frank and Dee Dee did their best to respect his privacy.

When Frank and Dee Dee were asked by concerned friends and family how the arrangement was working out, both of them answered "just fine."

Any problems?

"No. Not really."

Will it be hard for you two on the day that he leaves?

"Difficult, for sure." Frank and Dee Dee did their best to appear appropriately grieved. That's right. They would sure enough be all alone again. Just the two of them. It would be so hard.

They planned to console themselves by painting Chip's old room bright pink.

I met Dee Dee for the first time when I spoke at a recent women's retreat. When I stood behind the podium and looked out at the sea of smiling faces, hers was the one who caught my eye. And no wonder. Dee Dee was hard to miss. Crowned with a halo of fluffy white hair, she was dressed in a stunning red pantsuit, red lipstick, and red shoes. In her hair, right at the very front, was pinned a darling poufy red bow—the kind a little girl would wear to school or church.

When my talk was over, we divided into small groups. I was pleased when I saw that I'd been put in the same group as the woman in red. She looked like someone I'd like to get to know.

After the morning session, Dee Dee and I stole a chance to chat.

First off, I told my new friend how much I liked the way she fixed her hair.

She laughed. "People who don't know me think that I'm just a crazy old woman, wearing a bow like this. But the truth is, I *always* wear a bow in my hair. I've got them in every color you can imagine. Some of 'em are even bigger than this."

Those must be some very big bows, I thought.

"I suppose maybe I am a bit nutty, but there's a reason I wear my bows," Dee Dee continued. "My husband Frank died 20 years ago. We were very close."

"I'm so sorry," I said. "You must miss him a lot."

"Honey, you have no idea. He was only 58 and the picture of health when he dropped dead with a heart attack. It was terrible. Why, just the year before, we had gotten our last son raised and out of the house. We were just enjoying ourselves, having the best time of our life."

"We still have a child at home," I said. "I can't imagine what it's going to be like for my husband and me when we're all alone. I wonder if we'll even know what to do with ourselves."

"Believe me," she winked, "you'll figure something out."

I blushed just a bit. "So, what does your late husband have to do with you wearing a bow?"

"I taught school for 26 years. Junior high. I was still teaching when Frank died. After the funeral I took several weeks off. Folks were so good to me. All the boys came home, other family too. The neighbors came by and the members of my church just kept bringing food. But finally everyone went home, and the Monday morning came when I had to go back to school for the first time since Frank's death. I got up early, put my clothes on, fixed my hair, ate my breakfast, and had my daily devotional.

"Last thing, just before time to leave, I went into the bathroom to brush my teeth. I remember I stood there, looking at myself in the mirror. Who was I without my Frank? This was my worst day of all. How would I find the strength to face my students, the other teachers—to answer all their questions and manage somehow to act like I was fine? I tell you, it was all I could do not to get back in my bed and pull the covers up over my head."

"I can't imagine how you made yourself go."

"I almost didn't. The thought crossed my mind to pick up the phone, call the school, and tell them to find me a sub. Then I happened to look down on the counter, next to the sink. There was a cute pink hair ribbon that my great-niece had left by mistake. And all of the sudden I remembered old Noah and the flood…"

Noah? The flood?

"Remember how after the storm God sent a rainbow? Get it? Rain-b-o-w? He put that big rainbow over their heads to show Noah and his family how much He cared for them. Same as He cares for me."

"So you wore your niece's bow that day?"

"Yes. And again the next day, and the day after that. Soon I didn't feel right unless I had a bow in my hair. I never intended to make a habit of it, but it made me feel so much better. Every time I'd start to thinking about all I'd been through, I'd reach up and touch it and it would remind me of how God cared for me too."

"So now you always wear a bow?"

"Every single day. About six months after Frank died, I up and decided to go to school without one. I turned off the stove, unplugged the iron, locked all the doors, engaged the alarm system, opened the garage, got into my car, backed out onto the street, closed the garage door, and realized I couldn't do it. I went all the way back in after my bow."

"What a wonderful story!"

"I'm glad you think so. Not only are my hair bows a remembrance of God's care for me, they open the door for me to share my faith with others."

It was almost time for me to speak again. After thanking Dee Dee for spending time with me, I reached up and pushed my needing-a-trim bangs back from my face.

"You know, hon," Dee Dee's eyes twinkled, "a bow would look awfully cute on you!"

I have placed my rainbow in the clouds
as a sign of my promise until the end of time,
to you and to all the earth.
GENESIS 9:13 (TLB)

CHAPTER SEVEN

POPCORN
AND A COKE

Wise folks contend that opposites attract. If this fact is to be trusted, then the immediate connection felt by my now-husband Randy and me can most certainly be explained. After enjoying our first date, neither of us could bear to be apart from the other for more than a day.

When lecturing our own teenagers about the seriousness of choosing a mate, we've tried to fudge a bit. The truth is, so sure were Randy and I of our love for each other that within a mere week of our first date we became engaged. Five months after our engagement, we were married.

Such a rapid union, while terribly romantic-sounding to a pair of starry-eyed 20-year-olds, came at a high cost. Not until *after* the wedding did we discover the uniqueness of the person to whom we had each committed to live with for the rest of our lives. Possessing polar-opposite personalities—Randy, laid-back and easygoing, calm and quiet; I, organized and controlling, high-strung and vocal—we experienced predictable chaos during our first year of marriage. So stormy were those early months that I imagine our angels in heaven threw a celebration party and heaved great sighs of relief when our union unexpectedly survived one year.

But Randy and I did make it through that first year, and the second year, and the third one too. Today, after we've been married 22 years, being apart for more than a day or two makes us feel uncomfortable and uneasy. We've learned to be gentle with each other's idiosyncrasies and flaws. Every night, we fall asleep nestled together like a pair of plump puppies.

While our personalities remain very different from each other, some of the best of each of us has rubbed off on the other. I've found great relief in learning to relax, and in discovering that I don't have to be in charge of the world. Randy agrees that there are times it's best to stand up and speak up. No longer do I feel the need to plan the minute-by-minute details of our lives. Not so often does Randy leave important decisions until the very last minute.

And though admittedly I still fuss and fume over some of the things Randy does, mostly I've grown to love and appreciate his gentle, forgiving nature. Living with this man who is so blessedly slow to speak and slow to anger has taught me endless lessons about patience and the value of peace.

Ten years into our union, on a lazy Sunday afternoon, Randy and I sit hand-in-hand in a semi-darkened movie theater, waiting for the show to begin. It being Senior Citizen Discount Coupon Day, the theater is full of folks bedecked with bifocals and crowned with gray hair. In the youthful minority, on this afternoon Randy and I are likely two of only a handful of folks who have paid full ticket price.

Do we care?

Not a bit. Celebrating our anniversary, the two of us are savoring the delicious last few hours of a weekend getaway. We've enjoyed a wonderful two days. As soon as the last credits of the movie roll past, playtime will be over. We'll drive home, collect our offspring from my parents, and get down to the realities of another busy week.

We are in *no* great hurry to leave.

Before the show starts, the two of us indulge in a tub of salty buttered popcorn, two cups of soda, and a box of chocolate-covered raisins. Conspiratorially, we hunch down in our seats and savor the rare treats.

As we munch our snacks, time comes for the feature to start. It is past time actually, but the giant screen remains curiously blank. I check my watch. Other folks look at their watches too. Some of them get out reading glasses to make sure they're reading their watches right. The news is not good. Folks don't like what they see. No sir, they don't. All around us, unhappy moviegoers begin to murmur and complain.

"Harold, it's past one o'clock. Isn't it time for the show to start?"

"If the newspaper says the show starts at one, well, I think that it should start right at one."

"You think something's the matter with the projector?"

"If I remember right, the last time we came to this theater, the show started late then too."

"Someone could at least let us know what's going on."

Before long, trails of ticket-holders, mostly male, and mostly nudged into action by their wives, begin stiff-legged hikes up the aisle and back to the manager's booth.

Their mission? To find out what the hay is going on.

"Trouble with the projector," we overhear.

"They're working on it."

"Says the show should start in five minutes or less."

"What time is it now?"

"Now?"

"How about now?"

Five minutes pass, then ten. The screen stays blank, and the crowd gets rowdy—as rowdy, at least, as a bunch of senior adults dare get, considering high blood pressure, acid reflux, and such. More angry, arthritic, up-the-aisle treks are made.

Finally there is news. While the theater manager wisely cowers behind the locked door of his office, his assistant, an acne-afflicted, retainer-wearing young man, shuffles to the front of the theater. Head down, hands thrust deep into the pockets of his black double-knits, he explains that the projector is broken. A part is needed from the theater across town. The part is on its way, but likely it will be at least another half hour before the show starts.

Half an hour! The crowd cries for blood.

"I did not pay good money to sit here and wait."

"This is not right!"

"Something should be done!"

"I'll say!"

Easily swayed, I could be convinced.

Not Randy. I look over at him. He is calmly reading the sports section of the newspaper, unmoved by it all. Finally, turning the page he looks up, listens to the crowd's mutinous words for a moment, and wryly observes, "They'd best get this thing fixed, and fast. After all, these people have places to go—people to see—medicine to take."

We were so young and so very cool.

Now into our 40s (our *early* 40s, please understand), Randy and I are closer in age to the sensibly shod, elastic-waist-pants-wearing set than we are to those harried young parents we run into in the checkout line at the drugstore—where Randy and I both, by the way, get our prescriptions filled. The two of us have discovered, as we've matured, that prime-time game shows can be quality entertainment, that golden-oldies music sounds good to our ears, and that one should never pass up a chance to get a free blood-pressure check.

"What," we ask of our snotty kids, "is so *wrong* about occasionally eating dinner at four-thirty?"

"Yes," I tell my daughter, who fancies herself a member of the fashion police, "I *know* you think that high heels would look nice with my dress. Personally, I believe that these cute little flats look just great."

There is no doubt—Randy and I have crossed over from young adulthood to modern maturity, from two-door to four-, heavy metal to classic rock, the Young Marrieds Sunday School Class to Adult II. The way things are going, all-out geezerhood can't be many years ahead.

Looking back at that afternoon so many years ago, I finally understand. Those folks at the theater were right to get upset.

Life is short.

There's no time to waste.

It's way past time to get on with the show!

> *They will still bear fruit in old age,*
> *they will stay fresh and green.*
> PSALM 92:14

FRIENDS TILL THE END

PART TWO

CHAPTER EIGHT

VICTORIA'S SECRET

When Victoria Mullens became a Christian—while visiting her favorite out-of-state second cousin, Irene—she was advised by the nice minister who taught her, baptized her, and presented her with a brand-new monogrammed Bible, that when she returned home she should find a local church, attend all its meetings and services, and get herself involved in some area of good works.

Fine, Victoria thought. She looked forward to meeting new like-minded friends. She wanted to learn all she could about the Bible, and she certainly didn't mind hard work. Since the minister had neglected to explain how exactly it is one goes about finding a church, Victoria figured it out all on her own. Using the same method she employed when, new to town, she needed a plumber, a hairdresser, or a furniture upholsterer, Victoria went to the yellow pages.

Alpha Church of God in Christ…
Brotherhood Baptist…
Community Methodist…
New Hope Church of the Lamb…
Travelers' Rest Redeemer Church…
Zion Road Presbyterian…
Well.

Victoria had not expected so many choices. This was quite a quandary. Should she pick the one with the biggest advertisement? Visit each church and then decide? Study a city map to see which church was located closest to her house? She decided on none of the above. Instead, Victoria closed her eyes, took a deep breath, and let her fingers do the walking. When she opened her eyes, she saw that her index finger had landed on Charity Street Church of Christ.

Nice enough name, thought Victoria. Charity Street Church of Christ it would be.

It's been three decades now since Victoria came to be a member in good standing there, and she likes it as much now as she did the first Sunday she walked in. The people at Charity are friendly, the sermons are uplifting, and there is always plenty of work to be done.

Over the years Victoria has seen lots of changes come about in the ways the church goes about its business of saving lost souls. Never forgetting the good advice of the minister who told her to commit herself to good works, Victoria has kept herself involved in whatever happens to be the chosen church project or program of the year.

Back in the 70s, following the example of the much admired, rapidly growing congregations of the day, Charity Street Church of Christ committed itself to bus ministry. Every Sunday morning, Victoria and other workers boarded the Joy Bus—a repainted, refurbished school bus—to ride up and down the town's neighborhoods and streets, waking up, picking up, and sometimes cleaning up (early on, Victoria learned to pack combs, Kleenex, and wet washrags) little kids who needed to learn about Jesus.

Though it took weeks to overcome her natural tendency toward motion sickness—what with the old bus sputtering and spewing, lurching from stop to stop—within time Victoria became amazingly adept at holding on to the back of the front bus seat with one hand while teaching flannel-graph Bible stories with the other. (It was all in how you planted your feet, she once explained.)

The kids who rode the bus were crazy about Victoria, and she loved them back. In preparation for Sunday's bus rides, Victoria spent her Saturday afternoons baking cookies for the kiddos to enjoy on their way to church. Many of them would not have had any breakfast before boarding. They needed a little something to tide them over until lunchtime.

Besides, she'd learned early on that having a little something to nibble along the way soothed *her* fussy tummy as well.

Most churches change with the times, and by the early 80s—for a number of good reasons—bus ministries fell out of vogue. Though, like most congregations, they stopped running the Sunday-morning bus route, the Charity Street church held onto its commitment to children. In response to the plight of the many little ones who, because of working parents, had no one to greet them when they arrived home after school, on a hot September Monday in 1981, members of the church launched the town's first free latchkey childcare program.

The venture proved to be a huge success. Five afternoons a week Victoria and a dozen other dedicated folks provided after-school care to more than 70 children. Faithfully at the building between the hours of three and six, church members fed the children snacks, played games with them, held them, cuddled them, and nudged them into doing their homework.

When she was a girl, Victoria had loved school so much that she had dreamed of becoming a teacher. That never happened, but tutoring and helping the latchkey kids with their homework was what she liked to do best. Victoria loved good books, so many afternoons, parents arrived to find their children sitting in a circle at her feet, enthralled by whatever story they had chosen for her to read to them that day. She was glad the children most often requested a Dr. Seuss book. The good doctor was her favorite author too.

By the mid-90s, two notable changes had occurred at Charity Street Church of Christ.

First, over the past ten years, the neighborhood where the building was located had been experiencing a gradual but steady decline. Though 50 years before the church had been built on a half-block of prime real estate, now its vicinity was deemed by most young families to be seedy and run-down. How could you blame young people who chose to make their homes in the pretty new neighborhoods springing up along the outskirts of town? Folks assumed that these same young folks would attend churches located in their new neighborhoods. To do so was only natural.

The second notable change—and it was directly related to the first one—was that the membership (just like the population of the surrounding neighborhood) of the Charity Street Church of Christ had become an increasingly aged one. On any given Sunday there were more walkers parked in the foyer than strollers, and more worshipers using large-print Bibles than teenagers passing notes. At a recent deacons' meeting, it had been agreed upon by all that now a greater need existed for raised toilets in the restrooms than for additional breast-feeding chairs and diaper-changing tables in the nursery.

To its credit, rather than just lamenting the way things were, once again Charity Street church changed with the times, this time developing vibrant programs aimed at meeting the physical and spiritual needs of senior citizens. Calling upon the talents of its members, the church opened up both a food pantry and a clothing room designed specifically to meet the needs of its fixed-income members, their friends, and their neighbors.

Victoria, by then in her early 50s, worked two mornings a week in the clothing room. She, along with other workers, sorted, mended, washed, ironed, and hung the donated clothing up by size, season, and sex. It was amazing what anonymous towns-people dropped into the donation boxes outside the back door of the church. During the three years she'd spent at this work Victoria had seen everything from mink stoles and designer suits with the tags still on to blue-denim overalls so well worn that one could see clear through the seat.

It was understood that any member of the church was welcome to any item in the clothing room at any time—even if the day didn't happen to be a scheduled giveaway Tuesday. One of the perks of helping out in the room was that the volunteers got first pick at whatever nice donations came in. Victoria, difficult to fit, was pleased one year to run onto a perfect winter coat, tickled another year to find a pair of warm leather boots.

After years spent working together, the clothing room's dedicated volunteers could recite from memory each other's sizes. As the ladies companionably sorted through mounds of clothing, they kept their eyes out for each other's specific needs—a dressy dress for someone's niece's wedding, a raincoat for a lucky volunteer planning a trip to England, worn-out blue jeans for a crafter who used the scraps to make graduation quilts for her teenage grandchildren.

One entire winter, Victoria, curiously, kept her needs to herself. The reason? Though none of the clothing-room workers would have *ever* guessed, Victoria was on the lookout for skimpy lingerie.

It was a known fact that people routinely cast off such unlikely items as silk shorty pajamas, red satin push-up bras, and lacy bikinis. Such donations, though they made the group giggle, did not make it to clothing-room racks, and instead were quickly and quietly disposed of in the bin marked "trash."

Victoria, who had decided that she *needed* a collection of such things, found herself, after only a couple of tries, able to skillfully glean the delicate unmentionables without any of the other workers knowing she was doing so. Humming to herself, pretending all the while to be looking for her glasses, a cough drop, or a thimble, Victoria stuffed the secret items into her tote bag—where they would stay wadded up and crumpled until the end of the day when she would take them to her house—

Where she would save them.

For a special occasion.

Like the annual mid-May Senior Citizens' Retreat.

Victoria, though their junior by 10 years at least, enjoyed spending time with the over-65 set. She helped plan and orchestrate their retreat every year. Held at a lovely, rustic resort two hours from the church, the three-day weekend was an annual highlight for folks who didn't normally leave town. Planned with senior citizens in mind, concessions were made for frequent bladders and cranky hearing aids. The retreat center had few steps to climb and offered plenty of diabetic entrées to choose from at lunch. Adjacent to the main meeting and worship center, double rooms for men, women, and married couples opened onto a common hall. The only inconvenience? No bathrooms inside the rooms. Instead, showers, toilets, and sinks were located in two separate restroom areas, the men's at one end of the hall, the women's at the other.

It was in one of those bathrooms—the ladies' of course—that on the second day of the retreat Victoria pulled out her collection of clandestinely collected clothing. After making absolutely sure that the coast was clear—that all the retreat attendees were safely ensconced in the meeting room—Victoria proceeded to rinse the already clean items out in the sink, wring them out by hand, and drape them over a visible-to-all-who-walked-into-the-bathroom shower-curtain rod to dry.

First a sheer pink push-up bra.

Then a tiny black thong.

Next a silky baby-doll nightie.

And finally a leopard-print teddy.

When the session was over, Victoria, who had slipped unnoticed back into the meeting room, was among the women who raced to the restroom. She watched as each sensibly shod, pocket book-carrying, polyester-pantsuited woman made her way into the bathroom—innocently intent on taking care of just one pressing need—only to be greeted head-on by a startling collection of extremely racy underthings, hung right at eye level.

The women looked.

Looked again.

Looked away.

Said not a word, but cast sneaky sidelong looks at each other.

Not mine.

Not mine.

Certainly not mine!

Then whose?

No one spoke the words out loud. No one dared—not even the next day when, after stumbling to the restroom for their early-morning visit, the women were confronted by a fresh assortment of decidedly *unsensible* underthings.

Well. They had never.

Victoria, now well into her 70s, is a cherished friend of mine. Her energy, quick wit, and sense of fun make her one of my favorite lunch buddies. "So," I asked her over cafeteria pie and coffee, "did anyone *ever* say *anything* about the panty prank? Did you ever hear any of the church ladies discuss it among themselves?"

"Never did," she answered. "But wait till you hear this: Not too long after that weekend, I was shopping at the Sears just down the street from the church. When the salesgirl asked me what I was looking for, she acted surprised when I told her a plain white half-slip."

" 'Nothing else today?'

" 'No thank you,' I answered.

"Then the little girl confided to me that for the past month or so, the store had experienced an unprecedented run on skimpy underthings—black lace bras, silk bikinis, baby-doll pajama sets. (Remember, Annette, this is *Sears* we're talking about.)"

" 'You probably won't believe this,' the girl said, 'but it's the *older* ladies—you know, the ones with blue hair and varicose veins— who keep buying them up! We can't keep up with the demand.' "

"Why, imagine that," was all that Victoria could think of to say to the girl.

Imagine indeed.

Our mouths were filled with laughter.
PSALM 126:2

Chapter Nine

The Quest
To Be Normal

Kids grow up physically, mentally, and emotionally over the summer between their sixth and seventh years of school. Big changes take place. They mature. They become more independent. They leave many of their childish ways behind.

At least, most kids do.

It was during the first few days of his year in the seventh grade that Kevin Lederman realized for the first time ever that he was different from the other kids. That year, the one during which he turned 13, Kevin's buddies, one by one, began to leave him behind.

"Justin, wanna come play at my house after school today?" Kevin asked early on the morning of the first day of school. "I've got a new Nintendo game."

"Sorry, Kev. I can't. I've got soccer practice till five."

"Okay. Maybe you can come tomorrow."

"I'll have to see."

"Mitchell, *you* wanna come over?"

"Can't. I promised Missy Taylor that I'd go to her house after school. She's got a new dog. I told her I'd help her train him."

"I could come too. I know how to train dogs."

Mitchell looked at his feet, dug the toe of his shoe in the dirt. "Not today. Maybe next time, Kevin."

Kevin didn't know why, but after the first week of school, he no longer had all of the same classes or teachers as his old friends from sixth grade. He got moved to a different class. Except for PE and lunch, he didn't get to see his old friends all day.

While Kevin liked the kids in his new classes all right, he was relieved at lunch when, after two days in the new class, he spotted his old pals sitting together at a table in the cafeteria. Was this his lucky day or what? There was one empty chair. "Hi, everybody." He set his tray down.

"Hi, Kevin."

"Hey, Kev."

"Yo Kevin."

Though they greeted Kevin, so engrossed were his friends in a discussion about plans for an after-school football game—their heads bent low over napkin-sketched offensive and defensive plays—that when he sat down not one of them even looked up.

Kevin struggled to open his milk. He took a big swig. He swung his leg and coughed a couple of times. None of his friends were paying any attention to him. They were still talking about football. Kevin leaned over toward them. "Knock-knock," he said.

His friends loved knock-knock jokes. They always said that his were the best. When no one said "knock-knock" back, Kevin knew that it was because they hadn't heard him.

"Knock-knock," he said again—a bit louder this time.

Still no response.

"KNOCK-KNOCK!" Kevin screamed.

"Kevin!"

The cafeteria got quiet and everyone stared. He hadn't meant to say it *that* loud. He just wanted to tell his friends his new joke.

Mrs. Irby, the aide in charge of keeping order, hurried over. "Kevin, honey. That was a little loud. We have to keep our voices down when we're in the cafeteria."

Sheesh. He knew that. Mrs. Irby was talking to him like he was some kind of a baby or something.

"Let's pick up your tray and move over here to this table where the rest of your class is eating. Okay, sweetie?"

"But I wanna eat with my friends." Kevin looked to them for rescue, but they were busy staring at their plates.

"Come on, Kevin."

He got up and moved.

That afternoon when his mom picked him up, Kevin had some questions.

"How was your day?" she asked.

"It was fine."

"Hungry?"

"No." Kevin fiddled with the zipper on his jacket. "Mom, can I ask you something?"

"Sure."

"What's a 'retard'?"

His mom's knuckles blanched white where they gripped the wheel. "A *retard?* Where did you hear that word?"

"This kid in my new class said that everyone in there is a *retard.* He said we're all a bunch of *retards* and that's why we have to sit together at lunch."

Kevin's mom steered the car up into the driveway of their house. She turned off the engine and turned to her much-loved son. "Kevin, first off, there is no such word as 'retard.' Tell the boy in your class that he shouldn't say it anymore. The second thing is that part of what he said *is* true. The kids in your class are together because they, in one certain way, are all alike. You and the kids in your class have something in common."

"What's that?"

"It takes you longer to learn things. Like reading, writing—"

"And math?" Kevin finished.

"Yes."

"What about spelling? It takes me a long time to learn my spelling."

"That too."

"Okay. When do I get to go back to my old class?"

"Honey, you don't. I know it doesn't seem fair, but from now on you'll be going to class with other kids who learn slowly like you."

"For always?"

"For always."

"I wish I could sit with my old friends at lunch, Mom." Kevin suddenly started to cry. "I wish I had somebody to come play at my house."

"I know you do." His mother leaned over and gave him a hug. He buried his face in her embrace. "Just wait and see. I bet very soon, you'll make friends with the kids in your new class. Do any of them seem nice?"

"One does." His voice was muffled against her chest.

"Really, what's his name?"

"Jimmy. He wears things in his ears to help him hear." Kevin sat up. "Mom, they always fall off when he gets a drink at the water fountain."

His mother stifled a grin. "That doesn't sound good. So they get all wet?"

"Yep. But Jimmy don't care. He just dries 'em off on his shirt and puts 'em back in."

"Kevin, I'm thinking. You want me to find out where Jimmy lives? We could see if he'd like to come over and play one day this week."

"Yeah, Mom. That would be good."

By the end of the first semester of seventh grade Kevin and Jimmy had become best friends.

Kevin helped Jimmy keep up with his hearing aids. Sometimes they fell off and he didn't notice. When that happened, Kevin picked them up, wiped them on his shirt, and gave them back.

Jimmy helped Kevin remember to keep his voice down in class. Whenever he started to get too loud, before the teacher had a chance to get mad Jimmy would give Kevin the secret sign.

"Secret sign?" said Kevin's mother when she found out. "What secret sign?"

"Can't tell. It's a secret," Kevin solemnly explained.

Kevin and Jimmy stayed best friends all through middle school. High school too. When they graduated, their parents gave them a big party. They were both 20 years old and eager to be out on their own.

Borderline IQ.

Mentally challenged.

Over the years, Kevin and his friend Jimmy had heard the words again and again. Both of them knew that they were "retarded." Their mothers made sure that they heard the word at home. Their hope was that if the boys heard it often enough it would lose its sting, would not have the power to shame. Though neither comprehended exactly what *retarded* meant, what they understood was this: People treated them differently. There were things they longed to do but were told they couldn't—like drive a car or be University of Texas Longhorns. Some people didn't like them. A few people made fun of them. Both were smart enough to know there was a world bigger than their own, yet not smart enough to exactly fit in.

But oh, how they tried.

When they had turned 18, unbeknownst to their parents, Kevin and Jimmy had ridden the bus downtown to the army recruiting office and had tried to enlist. Kevin wore his favorite red cap, and together they tried to impress the uniformed man with a few of their favorite knock-knock jokes. Unfortunately, when they got to the punch line of one of their best, Jimmy's right hearing aid popped out, and the recruiter had to crawl under his desk to retrieve it. When it was kindly explained to them that perhaps the army wasn't exactly the best place for them to be, Kevin and Jimmy weren't terribly disappointed. They left happily, supplied with more free T-shirts, caps, and posters than they could carry.

In the fall after their May graduation, the two friends moved into a halfway house apartment, part of a unit designed for semi-independent adult living. This move marked the culmination of years of long-range planning. While they had been in school, their teachers had taught them a variety of life skills—how to cook simple meals, how to do laundry, how to manage a budget. At home, their parents had pushed them to practice what they knew. Moving into the apartment was Kevin and Jimmy's first try at independent living. This was their chance—the chance they had dreamed of and longed for—to show the world that they, even though they were retarded, were just like everybody else.

As residents of the apartment, Kevin and Jimmy were required to hold down jobs, to pay their rent and utilities on time, and to keep the place clean. Daily, for the first few weeks at least, they received a visit from Tom, the facility's resident life-skills counselor. Because he treated them with friendly respect, never once mentioning that they were different from anyone else, Kevin and Jimmy liked Tom a lot. They agreed that Tom was cool.

Tom was available to provide guidance, advice, and encouragement, to fix stuff, correct stuff, and to put out the proverbial fire.

Did I say "fire"?

On the first night after they moved in, Jimmy set a bag of microwave popcorn to smoldering when he set it to cook for ten minutes and went back to his room. Though no damage was done, they couldn't use the microwave anymore, and the new place smelled terrible for more than a week.

Just before the first day of their second month of independence, Kevin sent off for $400 worth of buy-one-get-one-free cassette tapes, and Jimmy gave his half of their second month's rent to a homeless man.

When they had lived in the apartment for three months, their toilet stopped up. Kevin and Jimmy, not knowing what to do, panicked. At the sight of rising water they flushed and flushed—more than ten times, flooding the bathroom and ruining all the carpet in the hall.

Every time there was a problem, Kevin and Jimmy had to meet with Tom to determine what they'd done wrong and to come up with a plan to keep whatever the situation was from happening again. Tom was generally patient and easy to talk to, but the meeting over the flood from the toilet didn't go too well.

After spending the better part of two hours plunging, pulling up carpet, and mopping up muck, Tom sat down to rest. "Guys, I know you're trying, but this just can't happen again."

Kevin and Jimmy hung their heads.

"We know, Tom."

"Sorry, Tom."

"You guys have just got to start using your heads. First there was the fire in the microwave, then the problem with your rent…"

Ashamed, Kevin and Jimmy both began to sniffle. Living in an apartment was harder than it looked. There were many things to remember, so many things that could go wrong. Maybe the across-the-street neighbors who said that retarded people shouldn't be living in the apartments were right. Maybe they really were dumb and stupid.

"Aw, Kevin, I'm sorry. I didn't mean to hurt your feelings," said Tom when he saw their tears. "Come on, Jimmy. You guys are doing fine. Everybody makes mistakes. I didn't mean to come down too hard on you. I'm just tired is all."

They were tired too.

Kevin wiped his nose on his sleeve. His shoulders slumped. "I guess we keep messin' up 'cause we're retarded."

"Naw, buddy, that's not it," said Tom. "You guys just need to be more careful is all. Next time you've got a problem and you don't know what to do, you need to come and get me real quick. That's what I'm here for. You come get me for any problem that you have. Deal?"

"Deal," they both agreed.

There was a long silence, then Kevin looked over at Jimmy. "Should we ask him about—you know—that *other* thing?"

"I guess so," said Jimmy.

"What other thing?" asked Tom. "Come on. I said you can ask me anything. Shoot."

"I don't know how to say this right," began Kevin. "It's just that every time me and Jimmy wash our clothes, we put 'em in the washer, and we put 'em in the dryer—"

"We *always* empty the lint trap like you showed us," Jimmy interrupted.

"But some of our socks don't come back. We look everywhere, but we never can find 'em."

"We look *everywhere*," Jimmy agreed.

"Tom," Kevin's face was pained, "do me and Jimmy keep losing our socks because we're retarded?"

Tom's face began to twitch. He rubbed his mouth with his hand. He looked at the ceiling and took three big breaths. He shuffled his feet and cleared his throat, but he could not hold it in. First only a couple of little snorts escaped. Then a medium-sized chuckle. Finally he let loose with out-and-out guffaws. Tom laughed so hard that he couldn't even talk.

Kevin and Jimmy looked at each other and wondered, *What now?* They weren't offended by Tom's laughter, but they wondered, *Should we call 9-1-1?*

Eventually, Tom got control of himself. He threw his arms across their shoulders. "Fellas, losing your socks doesn't have one thing to do with being retarded. Happens to everyone. Lemme show you something." He pulled up the legs of his pants to reveal one navy sock and one blue sock. "See?"

Kevin pulled up his pant legs to show that he had on one tan sock and one that was light brown.

Jimmy lifted the legs of *his* jeans. He had on striped tube socks. One had red stripes, the other green.

"You mean we're normal?" asked Kevin.

"Like everybody else?" asked Jimmy.

"Guys, you two are as normal as normal can be."

Relief flooded their faces. This had been a matter of grave concern.

"Whaddaya say we go get us a pizza?" said Tom in invitation. "My treat. Does that sound good?"

"Chuck E. Cheese?" asked Kevin with great hope.

"Why of course. Is there any other place?" answered Tom. "Come on. I'm starving. You two lock up and let's get going."

And so they did.

God chose the foolish things of the world to shame the wise;
God chose the weak things of the world to shame the strong.
1 CORINTHIANS 1:27

Chapter Ten

Need a Job?

When I was seven years old, my favorite uncle asked me what I wanted to be when I grew up.

What an easy question. "A missionary to Africa, a famous singer, and a veterinarian," I answered—not the least bit short on elementary-school–age self-confidence.

This morning I asked my husband what he'd wanted to be when he was a little boy. Randy told me that like most of his pals he'd dreamed of becoming a professional ballplayer when he grew up.

"Baseball?" I asked, recalling that it was his best sport.

"Or football," he replied. "Then again, basketball, golf, or even tennis would have been okay too. Given the chance, I wouldn't have been picky. Getting paid to play any sport at all would have been a dream come true."

Our university-student son, Russell, has known that he would be a teacher and a coach for as long as he can remember. A college junior, he's right on track. Not so his younger sister. Sixteen-year-old Rachel, aside from planning on being the mother of a houseful of children, hasn't a clue as to what job she will choose.

"Shouldn't I have some idea what I want to do when I grow up? At least a hint?" she frets.

"Don't worry," I tell her. "Give yourself some time. Once you're older you'll decide what you want to be."

I'm confident she will. Besides, even if Rachel did know now what she wants to be some day, in all likelihood she would change her mind between now and then. For it is a rare occurrence, I've observed, that childhood career dreams are fulfilled in the exact ways that we expect them to be.

Like many of our baby-boomer friends, the career paths that my husband, Randy, and I have followed have been marked by twists and turns, switchbacks and curves. Randy, at age 21, became a registered nurse. Later he went back to college so he could work as a high-school math teacher and a coach. Though he never fulfilled his dream of playing pro ball, coaching is something that he truly loves. For a guy gifted with only slightly-better-than-average athletic abilities, coaching student athletes has been the next best thing.

It was some time after age seven that I decided I liked people even more than I did animals. After high school, I studied to become not a veterinarian, but like Randy, a registered nurse. (You guessed right. The two of us met and fell in love while we were blue-smocked student nurses. What can I say? The man had a way with a stethoscope that took my breath away.) Last summer, after taking care of ill and injured folks for more than 20 years, I left nursing in order to write full-time. So far I've written five books, and I still have a couple more in the works.

If you were to ask, Randy and I would insist that, among our life priorities, our faith and our family come way before our jobs. Yet like most Americans, what we do to earn a living defines to others, *and* to ourselves, much of who we are. Our chosen occupations say a lot about us. Our work is important to us, and we take pride in what we do—perhaps too much pride.

Our family recently moved to a different community. The past few weeks we've been busy unpacking, finding our way around, and getting to know the friendly folks in our new town. As is nearly always the case when one meets new people, after Randy and I have gotten past all those basic introductions, we've found ourselves responding over and over again to the standard getting-to-know-you question "And what do you two do for a living?"

"I'm the new volleyball coach," Randy answers.

"I'm a writer," I say.

And finding our professions acceptable—admirable even—people say things like "pleased to meet you" and "welcome to our town."

Last spring, as I've done for the past dozen years, I traveled with a team of other Christians deep into the heart of Mexico on a mission to deliver free medical, dental, and spiritual care to the poorest of the poor. On our first morning of work, needy folks were already lined up and waiting when we arrived at the pre-arranged clinic site, a spacious, turquoise-painted, cinder-block church building. Desiring that no ill or weary person have to wait any longer than necessary, the well-practiced team members quickly unpacked supplies, set up the various clinic areas, and began directing patients through.

Late in the afternoon on that first day, indulging in a short break from my assigned tasks of blood-pressure taking and medication dispensing, I sipped a warm cola, leaned out an open church window, and enjoyed a few breaths of fresh air. From where I stood I could see down the street that ran in front of the church. I could study the shabby buildings and muddy yards and broken-down cars parked close to front doors.

Absently, still sipping my soda, I watched a family of four in the distance trudging up the street and toward the church. *Four more patients,* I rightly assumed. *Work's not done yet.* I finished the last of my drink. The family, from my vantage point, appeared to be a mom and a boy of about three, and a dad who was carrying a toddler in his arms. Arriving at the church door, the four of them entered, gave their names, and as instructed, took seats to wait for their turn to see the doctor.

It was not until I moved to greet the family that I saw that the toddler wasn't a toddler at all, but a boy of about six, disabled in some way. His eyes were vacant and set wide apart, his limbs long, spindly, and alarmingly thin. The child was limp, his muscles flaccid. Because he was unable to hold his own body erect, the boy's father cradled him like one would an infant, holding his son's head to his chest. While they sat waiting, the child's mother, sitting close, reached over and brushed a stray lock of hair out of his eyes, then straightened and smoothed the collar of his shirt.

Three out of four of them barefoot, all of them painfully thin, this family was poor—even by Mexican standards.

Arriving as they did so late in the day, I was glad that the foursome didn't have to wait long before being seen by a physician. Within a few minutes I motioned for them to pass on in to be seen. The doctor took much time with each member of the family and lingered long over the disabled son.

Once they'd had their consultations and received the free medicine that we'd brought to dispense, the family headed back down the street in the direction from which they'd come.

I speak only a little bit of Spanish, but many of the Mexican workers know English. "The little boy," I asked of the bilingual Mexican physician who had seen the family, "the handicapped one. What was his condition?"

"A metabolic problem. The child had it when he was born. He should have been given a certain special formula, but he did not receive it. Because he didn't get the formula, he suffered malnutrition and brain damage."

"Will he ever walk?"

"No."

"Does he speak?"

"No."

"Can he learn?"

"Sister"—my friend spoke with great patience—"the boy is like a baby. He can do nothing for himself. Day and night his parents must care for him."

"What if he got the formula now?" I asked, though I already knew the answer. "Would it help him?"

"No. It's too late. He needed the special formula in infancy, but his family had no money to buy it."

"Wages are very low here?" I asked.

"Yes, and jobs are scarce," the physician explained.

"What does the boy's father do for a living?"

"He is a…" The doctor groped for the right word. "The man is a…a…" He turned to another Mexican. The two of them conversed in rapid Spanish. Back and forth they spoke. I could not understand any of what they were saying. "Sister," he said as he finally turned to me, "there is no English word for the man's job."

No word? "Can you not explain?"

"He goes every day to the city dump to find things for his family. Food, clothes, items for their house. Sometimes he finds things that he can sell."

"That is his job?"

"Yes. He has no other. He does all that he can."

I've heard lots of good-hearted folks who, having made a mission trip or two, attempt to explain away the disparity between what they see in the desperate lives of the Mexican poor and the way that they, middle-class Americans, live.

"They're happy the way they are. Think of how much less stress they have than us."

"After all, they don't know anything else."

"Besides, how can a person miss what they've never had?"

I understand that the folks who say such things truly mean well—after all, they *have* gone and tried to help. I've said and thought some of the same things myself. For when one comes face-to-face with poverty, it's natural and human to need to explain it away, to try and gloss over the tragedy of it, to somehow figure out a way that it's really all right.

Even when it isn't.

I'm still very proud of the job that I do. I *love* telling folks I meet that I'm a writer by trade. I, of all people, have the coolest of jobs. But I learned an important lesson from the man who gleans from the dump to supply his family's needs. The job that a person does has nothing, *nothing* at all, to do with what he *is*.

For though there may be no English word for his profession, there is a name for *who* he is.

That name is *brother*. He is yours and mine.

And that is why I—along with a bunch of other well-meaning folks who, though clothed with the purest of intentions, will this side of heaven never truly understand—keep going back to do what we can.

> *He who is kind to the poor lends to the LORD,*
> *and he will reward him for what he has done.*
> PROVERBS 19:17

CHAPTER ELEVEN

COLORED EGGS

Funeral food.

We've all made it.

We've all eaten it.

King Ranch chicken. Banana pudding. Green-bean casserole. Sliced ham. Chocolate-cream pie. These are some of the favored funeral foods of my region—the South.

I'm sure it's much the same wherever you go, but we southern women take our funeral food seriously. We form food committees, keep running lists of who's to bring what, and routinely update our funeral-food phone chains.

The women of one church in a neighboring town even put together a funeral-food cookbook—not to sell, mind you—don't even *try* to buy one. The books were never intended to be fundraisers—rather the ladies put the volume together so as to streamline the process of providing a coordinated meal for people in need. Because of their forethought, when someone passes away, a preset plan of action is set in motion:

Jane? Can you bring page number 7? A double batch?

Ilene, we'll be needing page number 12. That's right. Eleven-thirty Thursday at the church.

Missy—call me if you get this message. We need you to make page number 3.

However it's done, all this organization serves an important purpose. In my community, within hours of someone's demise, a hot balanced meal, complete with dessert and iced tea, will appear on the bereaved family's kitchen table.

That's just the warm-up.

A death in the family calls for a two-to-three-day feed, especially if the arrival of lots of out-of-town kin is expected. Relatives can expect breakfast casserole, muffins, and juice on the morning of the funeral. Depending on the time the service is to be held, they may also receive a light lunch. After the actual funeral and graveside farewell, folks will be treated to a lovingly spread feast—food upon food, prepared at home, hauled to the church kitchen, reheated, dished up, sympathetically served, and of course cleaned up after.

Current wisdom informs us that it is our preoccupation with food that makes us fat. It says that if we are to be healthy and fit, we should learn to look upon food as nourishment for the body— nothing else. I suppose all that is true, yet when folks are sad, somehow they do find comfort in a pan of homemade yeast rolls. They discover there's love tucked into a bowl of tangy coleslaw. They feel a measure of peace when they take a bite of a strawberry-topped slice of cream-cheese pound cake.

And no wonder. Funeral food is nothing less than God's bounty prepared with lots of love and butter. It's not the food itself that's the greatest good, rather it's the servant heart of the folks who have prepared it.

My husband, Randy, cooks tasty spaghetti. He can also whip up a juicy hamburger in no time flat. I've even come home late to find that Randy has tossed together a salad. My husband, like other modern men when faced with the reality of a busy wife whose time and attention isn't spent 100 percent on the home, has cheerfully learned how to cook.

I actually think he enjoys it, and he's not alone. When I poll couples who have successfully divvied up household chores, I'm no longer surprised to learn that many men opt to take over the cooking in exchange for not having to help clean up.

Personally, I think men make *great* cooks. I see nothing wrong with men in the kitchen.

Except when it comes time to fix funeral food.

Bottom line? Cooking for those who have lost loved ones will always be a woman's domain. No matter how "liberated" or "progressive" we get to be, few women I know will give it up.

When we hear of a tragedy—say the drowning of a child, the death of a beloved husband, the passing of a dear grandmother—when any words we could say would ring hollow, when even hugs won't do, when there is nothing anyone can do to make the hurt go away, women know there is at least *something* they can do.

I've prayed while I made piecrust, punched out my grief over a breadboard, and salted beef stew with my own tears—all the while grateful that I was alone in my kitchen, thankful that the task of preparing food had fallen onto me.

Could I bring back the premature baby, the little baby born way too soon?

No. But I could take potato soup and carrot-raisin salad in a pretty glass bowl to the home of his 18-year-old mother.

Could I undo the car wreck that claimed the life of my best friend's father?

No. But I could make fudge brownies without any nuts—the way I knew that her twin girls like them best.

Could I reverse the ravages of cancer that stole the life of my Avon lady?

No. But I could deliver green Jell-O spiked with cottage cheese, pineapple, and chopped pecans to her children. When they saw it they would know that their mother was more to me than just a supplier of blush and eye shadow.

Love in a bowl.

Servants with spatulas.

Angels wearing aprons.

That's what you get with funeral food.

How fitting is this phrase, heard in many a southern mealtime prayer: "Lord, please bless the hands that prepared this food."

We had a death in my family a few months ago. An old person. A Christian. Someone whose time it was to go.

It was just after Easter Sunday. Flowers and trees were blooming everywhere. Soon as word got out, one of the church ladies called my mother's house. "Marolyn, tell me," she said, "how much family do you expect will come in? What time do you want us to bring tonight's meal?"

"That's hard to say," my mother explained. "Tonight, we'll have some of our children, our grandchildren, and a few aunts, uncles, and cousins all drifting in at different times. You know," she suggested, "we'll be fine without a meal. There's no need to bring anything tonight."

"Nonsense! You'll all need to eat. This is no time for you to have to be worrying about cooking. How about we bring over sandwiches, some chips and dips, cookies, and tea? We'll pop them in the fridge and you'll have something to pull out whenever folks get in."

"That would be wonderful," said my mother, truly tired and more grateful than she would say.

My brother and I were among those who were treated to that first night's spread. Living hours away as we do, we arrived late and hungry, but well after the funeral food ladies had come and gone. We dug through the fridge.

"How about a sandwich, Sis? Some chips?" My brother handed me a napkin and a paper plate.

"Sure. Sounds good. What kind do we have?"

"Let's see. Looks like ham-and-cheese here." He lifted a foil wrapper. "This is tuna."

"What about that big tray right there—what kind is that?" I asked.

He looked. "Egg salad, I think."

It was a huge tray. "That's a lot of egg salad."

"Sure is." He grabbed a half for himself. "I like egg salad. Do you ever make it?"

"Hardly ever. All that boiling and peeling—too much trouble for me." I reached for a sandwich too. Mmm. Good. Whoever had made the egg salad had done a great job. It was seasoned just right and spread on crusty, multigrain bread.

I wiped my mouth. "Of course when the kids were little, at Easter I never minded the time it took to boil eggs. I cooked dozens of them. Once they were cool, we dyed them and decorated them. Before church, Randy would get up early and hide them in the backyard."

"Did your kids eat the eggs after they found them?" my brother asked.

"Nope—what kids do? They were always too full from eating chocolate bunnies and marshmallow chicks to care about boiled eggs."

"So you just threw them away?"

"No, I put them in the fridge to use later, like for deviled eggs or chicken á la king. Sometimes I made egg salad"—I licked a smidgen from my thumb—"but mine was never as good as this."

My brother looked at me kind of funny, then glanced over at the tray from which we'd just plucked our meal.

"You don't think—" He grinned.

"Surely not."

"I bet you anything—"

"How many days ago was Easter?"

"Two. No, three."

"Let's see."

Gently, I picked up a sandwich and removed its top bread. Sure enough.

Colored eggs. If you looked real close you could see, mixed in with the yolks, the pickles, and the mayonnaise, bits of chopped-up whites, faintly tinted pink, green, and blue.

My brother and I shared our discovery with the rest of the family. They, like us, were amused by the frugal and festive filling. It pleased all of us to know that someone's leftover eggs didn't go all to waste.

Easter sandwiches.

Not exactly what you'd expect of somber funeral food. And yet, in light of what Easter's all about, keeping in mind what my extended family and I believe about life after death, about resurrection, about going to heaven and all, what could be more fitting?

Resurrection sandwiches. What a great idea!

I think I'll make a batch the next time *I* get a funeral-food call.

The eyes of all look to you,
and you give them their food at the proper time.
You open your hand
and satisfy the desires of every living thing.
The LORD is righteous in all his ways
and loving toward all he has made.

PSALM 145:15-17

Chapter Twelve

The Duchess Comes Home

When Chester received that year's pleading phone call from Camp Windy Pine's cash-strapped director, he didn't hesitate.

"Needing a couple more horses, are you?"

..."June, July, and August? Hmm. Let me think."

..."Well sure, Harvey. I reckon I can help out. In fact, I've got a little mare I'm not using right now. My wife calls her Duchess. She's getting up in years but she's gentle and real good with kids. When will you be needing her by?"

..."Friday of next week? Fine. I'll have her to you by then. And hey, Harv, will you be needing any tack? I've got a couple of extra saddles, maybe a spare bridle too."

..."All right. I'll bring them."

Camp Windy Pine, a summer youth facility dedicated to serving Christian kids, operated for ten weeks every summer. Along with Bible lessons, worship, and fellowship, campers were treated to cookouts, arts and crafts, swimming, softball—and horseback riding, which was one of the camp's most popular activities.

To save money (rarely did the facility operate out of the red), Camp Windy Pine did not keep its own animals. Instead, late every spring word was sent out to folks who believed in the mission of the camp and who were known to have horses. Some seasons it was easy to find enough loaners. Other years the camp's director was still making calls right up until the first of June.

A couple of days after receiving Harvey's request, Chester lured Duchess into the trailer with a bucket of feed. "Come on, girl. That's it. Easy. Step on up."

The process took a good ten minutes, for Duchess did not like trucks or trailers or travel of any kind. Only for Chester—not his wife, his son who lived on the ranch, nor any of the men who helped out—would Duchess even consider getting into the trailer without first throwing a noisy, tail-swishing, foot-stomping fit. But if it was Chester coaxing her, most times she would load without too much trouble.

"You're gonna do some work this summer, old girl. Be good for you." Chester slapped the horse on the rump once she was settled in. "Getting a little fat, you are. Sassy too. Okay, Duchess. Looks like you're all set." Chester cranked up the truck.

Duchess *did* work that summer. Four times a day, she and a dozen other horses were bridled, saddled, and mounted by jumpy youngsters, some of whom had never ever before seen a real steed.

They petted her nose. "You're a pretty horse."

They held their breath. "Pee-yew! Horses stink!"

They mounted on the wrong side, dropped their reins, and said *giddyap* when really they meant *whoa*.

Duchess tolerated it all. Unlike some of the horses on trail duty, not once did she buck or bite, or trot back to the barn before it was time.

It was toward the end of the summer that Chester received a long-distance call from the father of one of the kids who'd gone to camp. "Mr. Avery?"

"Speaking."

"Is this the Mr. Avery who owns a horse named Duchess?"

"Yes, it is. Who is this?"

"Mr. Avery, you don't know me. The reason I'm calling is to see if you would sell me your horse."

"Duchess? You want to buy Duchess?"

"I do. My little girl spent two weeks at Camp Windy Pine and fell in love with Duchess. Rode her every day. She's always wanted a horse. Once she got home she begged and begged me to see if I could buy her. Is she for sale?"

"I don't know." Chester was caught off guard. "I never thought about selling her. I've had her since she was a colt. You know, Duchess is a pretty old mare."

"That doesn't matter to me or to my little girl. She appears to be in good health. All my daughter wants is a horse to ride. Sir, I'm prepared to offer a good price."

With only a bit of negotiation, a deal was struck, and at the end of summer Duchess went to a new home. Since her new owner mailed him a check, Chester didn't even have to drive back to the camp.

Bet old Duchess put up a fuss getting into the man's trailer. Chester chuckled at the thought.

It may seem odd to those raised in town, but folks like Chester, who make their livings on farms and ranches, tend not to be too sentimental about their livestock. While they take good care of their animals—providing them with food, water, shelter, and veterinarian care—the cows, pigs, sheep, goats, and even the horses found in rural settings are usually valued not for their beauty or their personalities, but for the services or the income they provide to their owners.

Which explains why, though he felt a twinge of regret at the thought of letting her go, Chester didn't grieve over the sale of Duchess. She was past the time when she could safely produce more colts. At her advanced age, no longer did Chester pick her, from among the half-dozen horses he owned, to ride out into the pasture to check on the cattle. He had kept her for his city-dwelling grandkids to ride, but years had passed since any of them had requested that he saddle her up. Teenagers now, they were more interested in music and cars than in slow-moving nags.

So Duchess spent her days swishing flies and waiting for her lunch. Chester had planned to keep her around and, as he would with any horse, provide her care until the day she died. The old mare deserved that much. To do otherwise would not have been right.

But wasn't it better that someone, especially a little girl, enjoy her instead?

It should have been, but it wasn't.

Duchess had been gone for three-and-a-half years when, early one Saturday morning, Chester and his wife drove to a farm liquidation auction being held three hours from their place. They both enjoyed auctions. Sometimes there were real bargains to be had. Over the years the two of them had snagged great deals on everything from animals and equipment to antique dishes and furniture.

As they sped down the highway, Chester's wife asked, "Do you know the man who's selling out?"

"Nope," he answered. "Don't even remember his name. All I've heard is that he's fallen on hard times. Believe the man's got the bank breathing down his neck."

"Too bad for him, but that ought to make for some good bargains for us," his wife grinned.

"That it should," Chester agreed.

There *were* bargains. Lots of them. The sale included the contents of a house as well as a collection of farm equipment, numerous tools, and some livestock. The plan was that, by the end of the day, all would be sold.

At midmorning, Chester's wife purchased a silver tea set, some patio chairs, and three umbrellas.

Around noon, Chester successfully bid on a couple of barely used tractor tires.

Early in the afternoon, they joined several of their friends and neighbors—who'd also come to the sale—under a rented funeral-home tent where food was being sold. Chester paid seven dollars for a couple of barbecue sandwiches, four handfuls of potato chips, and two tall Styrofoam cups of sweet iced tea. Folks sat in folding chairs.

"Kind of sad to see a man's place sold out from under him," said one man.

"Yeah, it is," agreed Chester.

"Poor management?"

"That's what I hear. I don't know the fellow. Don't believe he's even here."

"He's not. I asked. Auction company's taking care of it all."

Around two o'clock the sale of livestock began. And though Chester had not brought his trailer, he and his wife stayed around to watch.

First up for sale came a chestnut mare. She was pitiful, old and sick, so thin that her hip bones stuck out. Her coat had the wooly, ragged look that indicated poor nutrition, maybe intestinal worms. Her feet needed to be trimmed. Dull-eyed and indifferent, she stepped into the auction pen with both her head and her tail down, seemingly unmoved by the unfamiliar sights and sounds that one would expect to startle or spook a healthy horse.

It was Chester's wife who recognized her first.

"Nah. It can't be."

"Honey—it is."

"But how—? What—? Why, she's in terrible shape!" When Chester became convinced that the horse in the ring *was* Duchess, he got hopping mad. "How could a man treat a horse like that, not take care of her, neglect her like that?"

Chester had no competition when he bid. He also had no way to get her home. His neighbor down the road, who *had* brought his trailer, offered to deliver Duchess to his place.

"Thanks. I'd appreciate it."

"Honey," Chester said to his wife moments later, "you ready? Let's go home." His mood was sour now. Hers too. Neither of them said much on the drive home.

When later that night, just before dark, Chester heard his neighbor's truck in the driveway to his house, he stepped out on the porch and watched them pull up. *Not much life left in her,* thought Chester. He could see into the trailer. Duchess stood with her head down and her feet still, seemingly unaware of where she was. *She may be blind. I wonder if she can still hear. Sort of looks like she can't.*

Then Chester backed the mare out of the trailer and something changed. The moment her feet touched ground, Duchess raised her head. It was like watching a resurrection. Her nostrils flared. Noisily, she sniffed and snorted the air, then the dirt at her feet, then the air again. Her ears jerked forward like a pair of darts and her tail rose like a plume. She reared her head back, tossed it to the side, and let out a loud, enthusiastic, trumpetlike whinny. Then she threw her head to the other side and let out another one. Then yet one more for good measure. If animals can smile, then Duchess sported a grin.

I'm home! she seemed to say. *Yippee! It's been a long time but I'm finally back home.* Then the old horse lowered her head, sniffed at Chester's boots, and let out a soft nicker.

At that very moment, it was determined that it would only be over Chester Avery's unsentimental old body—the one that had suddenly sprung two salty leaks—that Duchess would ever leave home again.

She never did.

Today Duchess is buried, I'm told, in the back pasture, in the easternmost corner of Chester's old ranch—a fitting place for equine royalty.

A righteous man cares for the needs of his animal.
PROVERBS 12:10

CHAPTER THIRTEEN

SPECIAL DELIVERY

Near the isolated farmhouse where I grew up stood some deep woods—more than 20 acres of them. When we were kids, my two brothers and I would play in the heavy green shadows there for hours and hours.

There we built elaborate though forever unsuccessful animal traps, collected pocketfuls of weird bugs, and stalked dangerous make-believe robbers and spies. An ankle-deep creek ran through the trees, and in its cool middle we'd wade, dig for freshwater mussels, and fish for crawdads. We built rickety fallen-branch bridges across the creek, raced leaf boats down it, and dug sticky, perfect-for-sculpting clay from its slippery wet banks.

Only when driven in by afternoon hunger pains did we appear in our mother's kitchen. Barefoot and smelling like a pack of dirty dogs, we either gobbled down our lunches or sweet-talked her into packing something for us so we could picnic in the woods. Always, there was important stuff yet to do.

One summer we formed our own construction crew. From my dad's barn, the three of us gleaned lumber, nails, a hammer, and a saw, and hauled it all into the woods. It took all of June and half of July, but with four carefully chosen trees as corner supports, we built a house with walls, a roof you could climb on top of, and shuttered windows you could stand and look out of.

This before any of us was 12 years old.

Those long days spent only in the company of each other taught my brothers and me to rely on one another and to make our own fun. Out of the earshot and eyesight of watchful, perhaps interfering, adults, and lacking the censoring influence of our peers, our imaginations found no boundaries.

Today, thanks in part to those solitary times, all three of us are free and creative thinkers. Though we've grown into responsible adults, my siblings and I have, each in our own way, chosen to live our lives somewhat outside of the box.

I can think of but one drawback to the way we spent our time as children. Having no close neighbors, no nearby library, movie theater, or corner store, we were sometimes lonely. We craved attention. Our hardworking parents took good care of us and gave us as much time as they could, but they, like all moms and dads, had lots to do. We three looked for playmates, for conversation, for something, *someone*, to break up our day.

Someone like the mailman.

Though other adults expected to be called Mr. or Mrs., our mailman let us call him Hank. We were convinced that he drove his route for the sole purpose of getting to see us every day. Dispensing letters, packages, and catalogs from a dented, dirty tan pickup truck, Hank arrived around noon, five days a week. Eager for his attention and affection, we watched and waited for his arrival with as much anticipation as our city cousins watched and waited for the neighborhood ice-cream truck.

"Hank's coming! Hank's coming!"

"It's Hank!"

Soon as we spotted him, on our toes we'd run out. The road would be scorching hot, so we'd hop from foot to foot, waving our arms and calling his name, determined to make sure he saw us.

"Here we are, Hank! Here we are!"

We three ragamuffins were hard to miss. Soon as Hank saw us, he'd stick his head out the window, holler his greetings, and nearly run his truck into the ditch waving at us. "Well, hello there, kiddos! How are y'all today?" Because he liked us so much, he'd stop his truck and let us climb in the back to ride the last half-mile loop of his route with him.

Our parents liked Hank, but much to their chagrin—being the dedicated civil servant that he was—Hank didn't stop at delivering the mail. He also brought us treats like raw sugarcane, out-of-date pastries from the day-old bread store, and animals—puppies and kittens, rabbits, and banty roosters that my brothers and I turned into backyard pets.

"Six roosters and no hens," my dad rightly complained. "What's the point in that?"

The brightly colored birds were a real trial to Dad because on the very day they arrived, the entire flock of them claimed the tree just outside the bathroom window as their nighttime roosting spot. Not all city folks may know this, but it's a rooster's God-given vocation in life to announce daybreak with as much noise and fanfare as he can muster. The Creator knew what He was doing, because the sound a rooster makes is a truly effective alarm clock—just ask anyone who's tried to sleep past dawn when there are roosters around.

Unfortunately, this particular bunch of birds took their roostering duties even more seriously than most. Every time my dad got up to go to the toilet in the night, they would see the light shining from the bathroom window, decide that the sun was coming up, and get all excited and wake each other up for at least an hour of nonstop crowing. After a number of sleepless hours, all due to the well-meaning critters' nocturnal confusion, my dad gave up and learned to take care of his business without turning on the light.

Toward the end of summer, by then having tired of the woods, and for the most part each other, my brothers and I united to put together elaborate backyard extravaganzas. Other kids dreamed about joining the circus. We started our own—complete with costumes, music and magic acts, trick animals, and free refreshments.

Who, it may be wondered, since we lived out in the country, miles from any neighbors, was our audience? Who watched our shows?

Why, Hank, of course!

On the summer days that we had a show prepared for Hank's enjoyment, the three of us never had to ask him twice to stay and watch. Never giving a sign that he was anything less than thrilled and honored to be invited to observe our acts, he'd pull his truck up in the yard, leisurely take a seat in the lawn chair specially reserved for him, and cheer and applaud like he had all the time in the world.

I don't recall Hank ever looking at his watch. He must have paid little mind to the fact that, once back at the post office, he'd have to explain to his bosses the half-dozen unhappy calls from folks up and down his route, folks who were irate and irritated because their mail was late.

No, as far as we could tell, Hank had nothing else to do.

In our show's opening act, wearing a one-piece bathing suit and a sequined headband, I twirled the baton while my brothers played the xylophone and sang "The Itsy-Bitsy Spider."

Bruce, buttoned into great-aunt Ella's discarded gold satin bathrobe, balanced himself on an upside-down plastic ice-cream bucket so as to be tall enough to serve as ringmaster. Not only was he ringmaster—Bruce was also the show's star animal trainer. He and his pets could do two tricks. For the first one, he twirled a crooked stick up, down, and around while his favorite rooster, appropriately named Tricky Mickey, moved his scaly feet forward and backward, managing somehow not to fall off the stick. After that amazing feat, Bruce's second trick, marching around the backyard with a different rooster perched on top of his head while Dayne and I drummed on empty tin cans, was a bit anticlimactic, but Hank applauded it just the same.

Dayne, wearing shorts, cowboy boots, and a bath-towel-turned-cape, was the circus's strong man. He amazed one and all when he broke one, then two, and finally *three* thick sticks into two—using only his bare hands.

When it was over, we treated the audience and ourselves to begged-from-the-kitchen ringside refreshments of Kool-Aid, marshmallows, and little boxes of Sun-Maid raisins.

We were sure that he meant it when Hank, rising to resume his route, would tell us again and again that our circus was the very best show that he'd ever seen. Even today, I'm still convinced that it was.

When my brothers and I reminisce about our old friend Hank, it isn't his mail-delivering skills that cause us to smile. It's not the gifts he gave us—the pets and the snacks—or even the rides he took us on.

When we talk about Hank, it's always about how much he enjoyed our shows. My brother Bruce still thinks it was his animal tricks that made Hank's day. Dayne is sure it was his strong-man act.

Me?

I'm positive that it was me and my baton-twirling that made Hank stay.

During Hank's tenure as a postman he delivered lots of mail—checks and bills, packages and catalogs. Some of it was deemed pretty valuable. The mail's timely delivery was important to him, but—as I look back—not as important as spending time with a trio of lonesome country kids.

I suspect that some rural-route residents didn't appreciate their delayed mail delivery. I know for a fact that some of them complained. However, I'll never agree with the statement that Hank tended to run late. In my mind, Hank was a man who always delivered on time.

I thank my God every time I remember you.
PHILIPPIANS 1:3

CHAPTER FOURTEEN

NO TALL TALE

I write stories for a living, but in my family the telling of tales didn't start with me. Whatever talent I have for turning the people and situations of everyday life into interesting vignettes I got from my dad. He's a great storyteller. And as is the case with all accomplished yarn-spinners, my dad's best stories, though rooted in real life, get bigger and better every time he tells them.

Confession? Mine do too. So accomplished are my dad and I that very few folks can tell which parts of our stories are true and which are embellished. Think you can? Give it a go. You'll not likely be able to.

Trust me on this.

There's only one drawback to being so good at what we do. Occasionally, people question and doubt us when we really *are* telling the truth! Even my dad and I know—no doubt about it— that there are certain times you've got to let the facts speak for themselves.

It was on a mission trip to Mexico that my dad and his good friend Henry—who, like Dad, was known to tell a tall tale or two—found themselves on the doorstep of a certain widow woman's tiny, dirt-floored house. On this particular afternoon, while the other team members dispensed medical, dental, and spiritual care, Henry and Dad hiked from house to house, from farm to farm, offering veterinary care to those folks who had animals in need of it.

One a rancher, the other a farmer, Dad and Henry were experienced in the doctoring of livestock. The care they offered was rudimentary—mostly oral medicine to treat common intestinal worms—but they *had* brought along a few doses of antibiotics and other more powerful medications to use should a situation arise where they needed to treat a really sick animal.

With no husband to support her, the young woman in whose crude house they now crouched—the structure's straw roof sagged too low for them to stand—was even poorer than her neighbors. Thin, dull-haired, and dressed in a frayed cotton dress, she stood there dull-eyed and downcast. Three young children, barefoot and hollow-cheeked, one of them perhaps blind, stood only inches from her side and stared.

The two men could detect no visible means of support for the woman and her children. None, that is, save a meager, nutrient-starved garden growing beside the house and a half-dozen scrawny chickens pecking for insects in the powdery dry dirt at their feet.

Politely, humbly, Henry and Dad asked the woman the same questions they'd been asking all morning long. Did she have any animals? Did she want them treated? They had medicine to give that would make her animals gain weight and grow stronger.

And it was free.

"Sí. Muchas gracias."

The woman had goats out back.

There were three nanny goats in the pen, all of them thin, but one so sick she looked ready to die. None of the goats were pets. The woman and her children *depended* on the gentle animals for the sustenance that came from their milk. Henry and Dad were correct when they guessed that, on some hungry days, goat milk was all that the little family had to quiet the churning of their empty stomachs.

"Best worm all three," observed Dad.

"Yep. They sure do need it." The goats were scrawny, wore the coarse, ragged coats that mark malnutrition—made worse by worms. As they prepared to give the medication, Henry motioned to the sicker goat, the one not able to stand. "That little gal's needing more than just worming. She's about gone, looks like."

"Yeah, she is. Doesn't look like she'll make it."

"Antibiotics?"

"Won't hurt."

"Likely won't help much either."

Both men agreed.

Henry gazed around at the sparse vegetation in and near the pen. "She doesn't stand a chance with nothing more'n weeds to eat. What I wouldn't give to have a bale of alfalfa hay with me."

"Wouldn't that be the thing," Dad agreed. "I've seen some of my sickest cows perk up on alfalfa. Some that I was sure would die have pulled through when I fed 'em alfalfa."

"Best hay there is. Sometimes better'n medicine."

"It is. Just a day or two on some good alfalfa would likely make the difference for this little one. It's a shame."

"It is. But a man'd be as likely to find alfalfa up here on this mountaintop as to find a pot of gold."

"I hear you."

Job done, they bade the woman goodbye, pressed a few coins into her hand, blew their noses, and headed in the direction of the next house, the next poor man or woman, the next pen of wormy livestock.

Which is where they found the gold.

"Is that what I think it is?" Dad pulled off his hat.

"Can't be."

"It is."

"I cannot believe what I'm seein'!"

"Where...how...?"

Alfalfa hay. At least two dozen bales of it, stacked against a neighbor's house. Never seen before—nor since—even coming up now on a decade of twice-a-year south-of-the-border trips.

"Reckon he'll sell it to us?" The two spoke conspiratorially, attempting to seem nonchalant behind the homeowner's back.

"Worth a try. How much cash you got on you?"

"Not much. What about you?"

They had enough.

Not only did the man sell them five days' worth of hay, he kindly assured them that he'd personally check on the sick goat and give the woman more hay if the goat was still sick. He gave them his word.

For a while, as they traced the half-mile back to join the rest of the group, neither man spoke. Finally: "No one's gonna believe us."

"I know it."

"*I* wouldn't believe some crazy story about finding alfalfa hay in this out-of-the-way place if someone told it to me. Would you?"

"Course not."

"Best keep this to ourselves."

"I agree."

So they did.

For all of ten minutes.

No big surprise. There was simply no way that a pair of story-tellers like them could be expected to keep a true tale like that to themselves for long.

I do not hide your righteousness in my heart;
I speak of your faithfulness and salvation.
I do not conceal your love and your truth from the great assembly.
PSALM 40:10

CHAPTER FIFTEEN

SNAKE IN THE GRASS

When Leland Masters was five years old, his mother took him and his seven-year-old sister, Jennifer, on an across-three-states car trip to visit Aunt Kay and Uncle Raymond. Leland's grandma on his daddy's side discouraged the trip. She did not think that it was wise for Mother to take off on such an adventure by herself.

"All I'm saying is, that's too long a trip for you and those little ones to make on your own," she chided Mother. In Grandma's day a married woman and her children did not go traipsing all over the country without a husband along for protection. "Something could happen. What if you break down on the side of the road? Have you given that any thought?"

"Yes, ma'am," Mother answered with respect, "I have. But I haven't seen my sister in more than two years."

"Can't you wait until sometime when James could go too?"

"No, ma'am. I've waited for him to take off and go but he stays too busy at work. You don't need to worry about us. I promise, I'll be careful."

True to her word, Mother was careful, and they made it just fine. Though the 14-hour station-wagon trip was tough on her, it was not so bad for Leland and Jennifer. Because Mother had put a foam mattress and lots of blankets and toys over the folded-down backseat, in those before–seat belt days the two of them were able to roll and tumble, sleep and play the whole way.

They did get tired of being in the car, but Mother stopped every couple of hours so Leland and Jennifer could go to the restroom and she could stretch her legs. Once they stopped for ice cream, and at lunchtime Mother pulled the station wagon into a roadside park where the three of them sat at a picnic table and ate pimento-cheese sandwiches, apples, and cookies, and drank icy-cold milk from the Thermos Daddy always took to work.

Finally, at just past eleven o'clock, Mother turned into the driveway and pulled the station wagon up to the house. "Leland—Jennifer," she called over her shoulder. "Wake up. We're here."

Aunt Kay and Uncle Raymond had, of course, stayed up waiting for Mother, Leland, and Jennifer to arrive. Though not really worried, over the past hour they had grown slightly anxious. As soon as Uncle Raymond heard the clunk of Mother closing her car door, he and Aunt Kay burst from the house with open arms.

"Well, hello there! Get yourselves in this house!" exclaimed Aunt Kay in greeting. "Thought you three would *never* get here!"

There were hugs and kisses all around, but after all those hours spent in the car, getting out and stepping into the bright light of the porch caused Jennifer to stumble and squint, and made sleepy Leland so suddenly shy that he hid his face in his mother's skirt.

"Any trouble on the way?" asked Uncle Raymond.

"You children hungry?"

"Thirsty?"

"Why, Raymond, look—they're tuckered out," said Aunt Kay. "You bring in their bags and I'll get them settled in the back bedroom. Come on, honey. Let's get you three to bed. We'll visit in the morning."

Before long, Mother was snoring in her bed, and Jennifer and Leland were asleep next to each other on a pallet on the floor.

Next morning, Leland woke to the smell of bacon and biscuits, to the feel of Jennifer's elbow in his ear, and to the sound of roosters crowing and baby calves bawling. Aunt Kay and Uncle Raymond lived on a farm. He had never been on a farm before.

After breakfast, while Mother and Aunt Kay washed the dishes and Jennifer took a bath, Uncle Raymond took Leland outside to see all the stuff that was on the farm.

He showed Leland the cows and the horses. Would he like to pet a baby calf? Ride the horse?

Not really. Afraid of animals, Leland held tightly to Uncle Raymond's hand.

Uncle Raymond took Leland into the barn. Would he like to play in the hay?

No. Leland looked at the ground.

How about taking a ride on the tractor?

No, thanks. Leland was a polite little boy, but honestly, so far nothing on the farm interested him one bit.

But then Uncle Raymond took Leland to the garden. When he spotted the straight rows of green plants on the other side of the fence, his face lit up, and he rushed over to get a closer look. There were tomatoes, peppers, corn, and squash; okra, cabbage, lettuce, onions, and more. "Wow!" Leland's eyes popped as he ran up and down the fence. "Is all this yours, Uncle Raymond?"

"Sure it is. Want a closer look?" Uncle Raymond opened the gate, and Leland rushed in.

"Uncle Raymond, what's this?"

"That's eggplant."

Darting to another row. "What's this?"

"Cucumber."

"And this?"

"That's a bean plant. See how it's climbing that pole?"

"Uncle Raymond, did you grow all this?"

"Me and your Aunt Kate did. You like to garden, Son?"

"I never tried it."

"Well, we'll have to change that. I'll be needing some help this week, picking and planting, pulling weeds and such. Would you like that?"

"I sure would."

"Fine. And when you and your mother go home, I'll send some seeds with you so you can make a little garden in the back of your house."

"That'd be great, Uncle Raymond!"

Uncle Raymond kept his word. At the end of the weeklong visit, during which Leland spent a good part of every day in the garden, talking, helping, asking about a million questions—generally getting in the way—Uncle Raymond gave him several little bags of seed and his own rake and hoe with the handles cut down to just the right size. At the time Uncle Raymond didn't realize it, but in giving such gifts to his nephew he was sowing the seeds of a lifetime.

When Leland got home, he planted those seeds in his mother's flower bed and got the biggest kick when they actually came up— little clusters of tiny green shoots. "Mother! Daddy! Jennifer! Come look!" He was even more thrilled when weeks later the plants grew tall and broad and began producing vegetables good enough to eat. When at supper the family tasted the produce that he had grown, Mother and Daddy and Jennifer agreed that Leland's were absolutely the best vegetables they had ever tasted.

As Leland grew older, his love of gardening grew too. When he was in the sixth grade, while his friends were playing baseball and riding bikes, he was tending a quarter-acre patch of dirt, studying seed catalogs for hours at a time, and pestering his mother to buy him a gas-powered tiller. By the time Leland was in high school, he had that tiller—and a lawn tractor too. Not only did he consistently win "Best of Show" at the county fair, but his vegetables were among those most sought after at the local farmer's market.

That was years ago. Leland is a grown-up man now, the head janitor at my daughter's school. Though he has the reputation of being an excellent worker, of keeping the school in really good shape, what Leland is really known for are the fruits, vegetables, and berries that he produces on his farm.

After all these years, the man *still* lives to work in his garden.

Leland has such a green thumb that every summer he ends up with more produce than can possibly be eaten by him, his wife, and even his three grown children who have big families of their own. As a result, he gives lots of what he grows away. Leland gives to the teachers at his school, to the senior-citizen center in town, to friends and neighbors, to strangers even—if he's had an especially good crop. So generous is Leland with the fruits of his labors that, towards the end of summer, folks at his church take to sneaking around and locking all their car doors out of fear that Leland will leave yet another paper bag of red onions, purple-hull peas, or Italian zucchini behind their front seats.

Last summer Leland decided to take on a new gardening challenge. After reading up, studying up, and chatting on-line with gardeners from coast to coast, he began experimenting with growing a number of little-known, rare, and exotic varieties of tomatoes. To no one's surprise, Leland's efforts proved successful—so much so that at the peak of the season he had close to 20 different varieties thriving in his patch. The healthy plants bore fruit that ranged from the tiny cherry-sized up to a few giants that by maturity had reached nearly the circumference of ripe cantaloupes. There were, in Leland's special patch, dark red tomatoes, light red tomatoes, yellow tomatoes, and even some tomatoes that were best harvested when they were still green.

That tomato patch was rightfully Leland's pride and his joy, which is why, during the months of June, July, and August, anyone who came to his house was treated to a guided, in-depth garden tour. It almost got to be a joke among those who liked Leland best. For no matter who you were—a friend, a relative, even an unsuspecting stranger stopping to ask for directions—if Leland was at home, you *were going* to get the tour.

It was during the middle of August, when Leland's crop was at its peak, that his two best friends, Jerald and Ray, stopped to pick him up for a morning of golf. Though he knew better, Ray pulled his truck up into the driveway and honked to let Leland know they were there.

Golf bag in hand, Leland stepped out his front door. "Wait a minute, fellers. Kill your engine, Ray, and y'all get out for a minute.

I want to show you something. Come on out to my garden. I've got something you'll want to see."

Indulgingly, Jerald and Ray got out and followed Leland out back. Frequent visitors—though they'd hoped to get to the course before ten—they knew now to expect the grand tour, 30 minutes at least, and that only if it ended quick.

"See this little gal here?" Leland pointed to a favorite specimen. "I ordered her from California. Have you ever seen a tomato with that kind of shape? Every one she puts out looks just like that. And look over here; this big beauty makes a fruit nearly as big around as a dinner plate."

It was about then that Leland's wife stuck her head out the back door and called for him to come to the phone. "Be right back," he assured them as he sprinted toward the house. "You guys feel free to look around all you want."

Honestly, Jerald and Ray wanted to play golf. *Today.* So while Leland was gone, they stepped outside the garden fence and hatched the perfect plan. The pair of them had it all cooked up by the time their friend got off the phone.

"You're not going to believe what we saw in there," Ray told Leland after he'd come back out. He and Jerald, outside the fence, both pointed toward the middle of Leland's prize tomato patch.

"Oh, Leland," added Ray, "it's not good."

"What are you talking about?"

"In the garden—"

"Between the second and third rows—"

"We saw a snake—"

"A big snake—"

"At least this long!" Ray spread his arms wide.

"You're kidding, right?" Leland had turned pale.

"No. Really. He was all curled up—"

"Right ready to strike."

"But we didn't wait around to see what he would do. No sirree. Me and Jerald got ourselves out of there fast!"

Leland, who at 240 pounds was scared *to death* of snakes, looked ready to cry.

"You *sure* it was a snake?" he whispered. "Not just a really big *worm?*"

"No doubt," Ray insisted.

"Man alive." Leland shook his head. "A snake in my garden. If that don't beat all."

After a moment, Ray had a bright idea. "Leland, what do you say we head on over to the course, play a round or two, and have us a hamburger in the clubhouse. Likely that snake'll be long gone by the time we get back."

Leland didn't feel much like playing golf anymore, but he got into Ray's truck anyway, and the three of them headed out to the course.

When they returned, hours later, Jerald and Ray started to get out at Leland's house. "You guys coming in?" he asked.

"We figured we'd go get our look at the garden now," answered Jerald.

"Yeah. Since we didn't get to see it all this morning," added Ray, feeling the slightest twinge of dirty-dog, lying guilt.

No way.

"You boys can do what you want to, but I'm not going anywhere near where that snake was. Even if he's gone, I hear they travel in pairs, family groups even. Why, by now there's probably a whole nest of them who've set up housekeeping in my tomato patch. No way I'm going back in there."

"You mean ever?" asked Ray.

"Never?" repeated Jerald.

"Heard me right," said Leland.

"Then how you planning on tending to it?" asked Jerald.

"I'm not."

"Aw, Leland. Come on, now. You mean to tell me that you'd let one little old snake ruin your garden for you?"

"I thought you said he was a big snake."

"Well, he was," started Ray.

"Pretty big," finished Jerald.

"Maybe not *that* big," said Ray.

"Don't matter. I'm not going back in there."

Ray looked at Jerald and Jerald looked at Ray. "Leland…," Ray said, digging the toe of his shoe in the ground, "we were just kidding you."

"There wasn't no snake. We just wanted to get goin' is all," said Jerald.

"That's right. There wasn't no snake," agreed Ray.

Leland would have none of that. "Don't be trying to fool me now. I know you two saw a snake and I'm not going back in there."

"But really—we didn't."

"Honest. There was no snake."

"Nice try," said Leland. "Appreciate what you're trying to do and all, but it don't change nothing. I'm not going back inside that fence."

And he didn't. No amount of confessing and convincing would change Leland's mind. There were a couple of times that he came close to thinking that Jerald and Ray might be telling the truth about there not being any snake, but what if they weren't? His mother did not raise a fool, and Leland decided not to take any chances.

Those prize tomatoes rotted on the vine. The big ones, the little once, the ones with the unusual shape. Went to waste. Every one of them. Leland never set foot in that garden again.

Poor Leland.

I relate to him so well.

Like him, sometimes the loose words of my friends stir up all kinds of crazy doubts and fears. *I'm not up for this task. I'm sure to fail. Who am I to think I can accomplish something like this?* Once I get going, as if of its own accord my imagination runs wild. Though I know better, I start to fear things I cannot see, to anticipate problems that *might* be, to become suspicious of snakes that *could* be—*might* be—lurking in the grass.

So what do I do?

Give up?

Leland didn't. For though he never did go back into that particular tomato patch, he did not stop gardening. Instead, after a few days time, Leland simply moved over a hundred yards and started tilling up a new patch.

When a person is faced with a problem they can't get past, a fear that won't go away, my friend Leland offers some helpful advice:

Leave the old place—the one that *might* contain a snake—behind.

Move over a short little piece.

Get back to work.

Don't waste time worrying about the past.

But just in case—it's never a bad idea to wear thick garden gloves!

As the soil makes the sprout come up
and a garden causes seeds to grow,
so the Sovereign LORD
will make righteousness and praise spring up before all nations.
ISAIAH 61:11

JUST KIDDIN'
AROUND
PART THREE

CHAPTER SIXTEEN

REAL MEN

"Whaddaya wanna do?"

"I don't know."

"I'm bored."

"Me too. There ain't nothin' to do."

"Sure ain't."

"I thought of something. Look up there. See them buzzards? Let's lay down and pretend like we're dead."

"How come?"

"So they'll fly down and land on our heads. Then we can grab 'em by their legs!"

"That's a great idea."

But though brothers Todd and Mark lay very, very still, trying their best to impersonate roadkill, not one single buzzard flew their way. After a long ten minutes, the two of them sat up at the same time. "That ain't gonna work," said Todd. "Let's think of something else to do."

"Wanna see if Nathan can come over?" Mark suggested.

"He's such a baby," said ten-year-old Todd. "Always trying to act tough, braggin' about how fast he can run, how he can beat some stupid little kid up."

"At least it'd be something to do," said Mark, who, though a head taller, at nine was Nathan's same age.

"Hey, I've got an idea. Let's get him to come over so that we can play a trick on him!"

A trick? What kind of trick?

Todd went inside to use the phone to call Nathan to see if he could come over. Nathan, of course, had to ask his mother for permission, but since she knew that Todd and Mark were such good boys, she immediately said yes. When Nathan arrived with money in his pocket, removing the necessity for Mark and Todd to extort cash from their mother, it was as if their plan had been divinely set.

Within minutes of Nathan's arrival, the three of them set out for Joe Ed Larkin's convenience store to buy cold drinks. It was about a mile walk down the country road. They took it slowly, allowing plenty of time for important stuff like spitting and playing kick the can. Once they made it to the store, after much discussion the boys decided to purchase a bag of Chee-tos, a pack of Big Red gum, and some Nu-Grape sodas. Nathan was going to get only one soda, but when he saw that Mark and Todd planned to consume two apiece, he, not to be outdrunk, opted for a second soda too.

On their way back, the three of them ate and drank as they walked. They were almost back to the house when Todd said, "Man, drinking those sodas made me have to *go*."

"Me too," agreed Mark. "I gotta go bad."

Though Nathan had only drunk part of his first soda, he was not about to be outdone. "I gotta go too. Grape always makes me hafta go."

Todd shot a sidelong glance at Mark. "Hey, Todd, why don't we let Nathan take the test."

"What test?" asked Nathan.

"The test that proves you're a man," said Todd. "Whatcha think, Mark?"

"I'm not sure. He may not be ready," said Mark.

"Shoot. I'm ready. I'm as much a man as you guys are. Come on. Show me the test. I can pass any test you guys got. Just give me a chance."

"Okay," said Todd. "We gotta go behind the barn."

Nathan followed along.

"See this wire fence? Don't get too close, 'cause if you touch it you'll get shocked."

"So what," said Nathan. "Big deal. That ain't nothing. I've seen an electric fence before. Lots of times. My granddad's got one at his farm."

"Sure, you've *seen* an electric fence, but have you ever *gone* on one?"

"You mean…?"

"Yep. On the wire."

"But won't you get a shock if you do?"

"Only if you can't go hard enough."

"To keep from getting shocked you have to go real hard."

"As hard as you can."

"Like this. Watch me and I'll show you how it's done." Todd, feigning great concentration and strength, produced a steady yellow stream.

Nathan watched in wonder but said not a word.

"See, I didn't get shocked. That's because I'm a *man*."

"It's my turn now," said Mark. "Watch this. I'm not a bit afraid. I'll go right on the wire." And he did.

"So Nathan—you still wanna try?"

"Well, yeah. Sure. I mean if you guys can do it, I can too. Just give me a minute to get ready. Almost. No. Not yet. Okay. Wait. Uh—okay. Now I'm ready." Sweat rolled down his face. Finally, he planted his feet, drew a deep breath, and took mighty aim. "Here goes."

Unseen, Todd, during all of Nathan's getting-ready time, had slipped quietly into the barn. At precisely the right instant, at a prearranged hand signal from Mark, he flipped the electric fence switch from OFF to ON.

What came next was quite a shock.

Todd and Mark and Nathan are grown-up men and good friends to this day. They look back at their childhood days and laugh about all the fun they had, the pranks they played, the tall tales they told each other.

As a nurse in the doctor's office where they came for their checkups, their flu shots, and their insurance exams, for years I was privy to an interesting fact about each of these men.

When it comes to the getting of a "specimen," I learned from the very beginning to allow each of them some extra time behind the locked restroom door. The reason? Apparently since childhood, they all have been plagued with "shy" kidneys!

You will surely forget your trouble,
recalling it only as waters gone by.
Job 11:16

CHAPTER SEVENTEEN

BAD WORDS

Seventeen boys and only five girls? This can't be right. Having arrived early on Monday, the first of the three teacher workdays scheduled prior to the fall starting of school, kindergarten teacher Esther Vaughn strolled into her principal's office. Holding the obviously erroneous roster in her hand, full of confidence, she queried her boss. "Mr. Martin, there seems to be a mistake. Could you take a look at this list?"

Mr. Martin, worried and preoccupied at the moment about threatening reports of a territorial skirmish between the janitorial staff and the lunchroom ladies, a shortage of health books, a delayed shipment of copy-machine paper, *and* in great need of a dose of caffeine, cast only the quickest of glances at the list Esther thrust under his chin. "No mistake."

"Seventeen boys?"

"That's right." Esther watched as Mr. Martin fumbled for something in his desk drawer. "Do you have change for a dollar? I'm dying for a Dr. Pepper and the machine's out of change."

"Sure," Esther scooped four quarters from her pocket. "What about Miss Annie Rae's class? How many boys does she have?" *This had better be fair*, Esther thought.

"Eighteen," answered Mr. Martin. "Beats all, doesn't it? Must have been something in the water that year. I for one have never

121

seen so many boys in one grade level. Do you realize that ten years from now we'll have one of the best football teams in the district?"

Well, all right then.

It was not that Esther had anything against boys, you understand. Actually, she adored them, having grown up with five brothers, and being this year in the big middle of raising two sons of her own. Problem was, knowing boys as she did, and being the experienced teacher that she was, Esther knew what to expect from them. Such an imbalance of the sexes in a classroom would definitely set a certain tone.

Over cheesecake and coffee, she discussed her class makeup with her friend, Jo, who was not a teacher— "It's just that boys are so…"

"…loud?" finished Jo.

"Yes, and…" Esther groped for words.

"…dirty?"

"Uh-huh, and…"

"…rowdy?"

"That's it!" agreed Esther. "And you know that even the best boys tend to…"

"…fight?"

"Yes, and…"

"…curse?"

"Yes, and…"

"…spit. Don't forget that boys love to spit."

"How could I forget?" Esther said. "I think it's the spitting that I hate the most."

"Looks like you're going to have an entire year to get used to it!"

Jo was right.

Seventeen boys and only five girls *did* make for a wildly active classroom. Esther loved all 17 of her smelly little sweethearts— and the girls too, of course. Yet every single day brought some new challenge. So demanding was teaching this year that about twice a week she wondered if she should have followed her mother's advice about becoming an accountant.

"Justin, please do not stand on top of the sink."

"Austin, I've asked you before not to stuff your snack crackers into the VCR."

"Sean! Wait! Don't pour your pencil shavings into the aquarium!"

And what was it with boys' fascination with body fluids? One afternoon, on recess duty, Esther noticed a dozen of her boys standing in a circle studying something in the dirt.

"Look at that!"

"Yuck! Gross!"

"Pee-yew!"

"Hey! What are you boys looking at? Let me see." Esther walked over to where the bigger part of her class stood. At her bidding, the circle parted—but then she wished it had not.

"It's throw-up, Miz Vaughn. See? Eric threw up. There's the hot dogs he had for lunch…and the chips he had for snack…"

No doubt. There they were.

The thing about a classroom full of boys is that to maintain order, a teacher must stay extra alert the entire day, Esther explained to Jo. At no time can she turn her back or let down her guard. If she does, someone might start a fire. Or a flood. Or worse!

Yet on occasion, a teacher needs to be in two places at once. Say, for instance, during the times set aside for students to take their water-fountain breaks. This is how it works: While some students stand in the hall waiting for their turn, others, thirst quenched, skip on back to the classroom. Esther has learned that if she allows the children—this year's class at least—to go unmonitored to get their drinks, inevitably someone will push, someone will shove someone else's face in the water, and a fight will break out.

Yet if she stands guard right next to the fountain, there is no telling what kind of stunt the students already back from their drinks will pull in her room. So, doing the best she knows how, every day during break time, Esther posts herself halfway between the two doors and hopes for the best.

At her hallway post last Friday it was business as usual, "Joey, don't put your mouth on the spigot."

"That's enough, Jonathan—let someone else have a turn."

"Keep your hands to yourself, Nick."

"No, it's not time for recess yet."

There were only two children to go when Esther saw Pedro, who had already had his drink, come tearing out of the classroom. "Miz Vaughn, Miz Vaughn, you better come quick!"

"Pedro, go get back in your seat," Esther scolded.

"But Miz Vaughn, you gotta come see! Charlie scratched a really bad cuss word on the back of Edward's seat!"

It was near the end of the year. By now, Esther was not surprised by much. Less than five minutes later, when she returned to her room, Esther found her students not in their seats, but crowded around Edward's carved-upon seat, each offering up dire predictions as to what Charlie's punishment would be.

"I bet you have to go to the principal's office."

"But I didn't do it," said Charlie, denying everything.

"I hear she gives you licks."

"I said I didn't do it."

"They might even kick you out of school!"

As Esther approached, Charlie laid his head on his desk, effectively blocking Esther's view of the word in question.

Esther took control of her class. "Sit down. All of you. Now! Charlie, I need to see what you've done."

"I didn't do nothing." His head stayed down.

"Charlie."

The little boy started to cry.

"Come on, now. Let me see."

Finally, he raised his head and Esther could see the bad word. P.I.S.D. In perfect block letters.

P.I.S.D.?

When Esther remembered, she had to struggle not to grin. Just yesterday in a faculty meeting, Mr. Martin had informed her and the other teachers that the school had, that day, received a shipment of donated used desks. They were told to expect current classroom desks in need of repair to be replaced—by the janitorial staff at night—with some of the donated desks.

And the source of the donations?

*P*ressland *I*ndependent *S*chool *D*istrict.

Charlie didn't get into trouble. Esther saw to that. She took up for him, stood him beside her in front of the class, and gave the rest of the students a stern talking to about accusing other students of something they didn't do.

That evening, chatting with Jo as they jogged laps at the track, Esther relayed the day's funny events. "I tell you," she confided, "sometimes after a crazy day with those kids, I wonder what I'm doing teaching school."

Jo laughed. "Well, looks to me like you've done one thing right for sure."

"What's that?" Esther asked.

"Those kids do know their phonics!"

Sure enough they do. If you happen to see Charlie, put Esther's teaching abilities to the test. Go ahead—ask him. Say, "Charlie, how do you spell Mrs. Vaughn's name?"

Nine times out of ten, he'll get it right: *L-U-V.*

Folks who know say that the key to teaching phonics is to simply have kids spell things the way they sound. I'd say Esther has it down pat.

A word aptly spoken
is like apples of gold in settings of silver.
PROVERBS 25:11

CHAPTER EIGHTEEN

KEEPING WATCH

"What a beauty!" With his eyepiece in place, 25-year-old Alex Garrett, redheaded owner of the newly opened Downtown Clock and Watch Shop, had no trouble looking past the deep dents and scratches in his customer's antique pocket watch. He could see its true worth.

"Thank you. It means a great deal to me," said the customer.

"Looks to be around 85, maybe 90 years old. How long have you had it?"

"Sixty-five years," the customer answered. "My uncle gave it to me when I was a ten-year-old boy. He bought it for himself but never could get used to carrying it. Since I pestered him to let me see his watch every time we were together, he knew I liked it. I suppose that's why he gave it to me."

"Not working?"

"No. Stopped a couple of months ago." While Alex leaned over the counter and examined the watch, the man shifted his feet. His eyes took in the sparseness of the tiny shop, and he squinted, trying to read the certificate that hung on the wall above Alex's bent head. "Son," the man finally asked, "you're not from around here, are you? Exactly how long have you been working on watches?"

Alex straightened up. New to this small town, he was used to folks questioning his age, and he took no offense. "Five years, sir.

I started trade school right after I graduated from high school. In Oklahoma. Finished fifth in my class. I can give you references if you want."

"No need of that." The man was reassured. "Can my watch be fixed?"

"I'll do my best. Could you check back in about a week?"

Repairing the man's watch was not a complicated or particularly difficult task. It took Alex less than a day to get the timepiece back in running order. He cleaned it, adjusted it, and replaced the single, tiny, worn-out part that was the cause of the trouble. Sadly, however, the watch, though in excellent shape on the inside, was terribly beat-up and worn-looking on the outside. It was Alex's pregnant wife, Jill, helping him out in the shop, who first suggested that he work out the dents.

"What a shame!" She held the piece in her warm palm. "Such a nice face. Pretty hands too. But all these dents. Is it a good watch?"

"A really good one."

"Kind of looks like it went through the clothes dryer or something, doesn't it?" said Jill.

Alex agreed.

"Couldn't you smooth it out a bit?"

He had not considered that. "Maybe. I don't know. It'd take a lot of time and I don't know how much good I could do. The customer and I never discussed any cosmetic work. He just asked me to clean it and get it running for him. The man might not want to pay extra for me to do more work."

Jill held the watch up by its chain and watched it twirl. "So what if he doesn't pay? You've got the time. If you fixed it up he'd probably be so surprised and pleased that he'd recommend our shop to all his friends. How many times have you said that the best way to build up the business is to satisfy your customers?"

She had an excellent point.

"I guess it won't hurt to see what I can do."

And so off and on for the next three days, Alex worked on those dents. He smoothed and polished, pressed and shaped. Gradually, the dents became less and less noticeable. The scratches almost polished out.

Jill approved. "Alex! It looks so much better! That man is going to be shocked. I do hope I'm here when he comes to pick it up. I want to see his face. You know, I bet he won't even recognize his own watch when he sees it!"

Jill was absolutely right. And she was in the shop to see for herself.

"Son, you've made a mistake," said the customer on the day he came to pick it up. "This isn't mine."

"Sir, it is your watch." Alex and Jill flashed smug smiles at each other.

"My watch had lots of dents in it. This one looks almost new."

"I worked on it all weekend long. Cleaned it up, polished it up. I figured you wouldn't recognize it when you saw it."

"But…" The man fell silent.

Alex beamed. This was even better than what he'd thought. His customer was so pleased that he was speechless. Jill had been so right. "Don't worry, sir, there's no charge for the extra work. Why a nice watch like that—it was my pleasure."

The man stood there staring at the watch, turning it over and over in his hand. "What happened to the dents, to all the scratches?"

"I smoothed them out for you. It wasn't so hard."

The man looked some more.

"Is something wrong?"

For a long moment he did not speak. Finally, with a trembling chin—"I've got six grandchildren. All of them grown now. But from the time each one of them was born, I would hold them in my lap during church and let them play with whatever I had in my pockets—you know, my keys, my fountain pen, even my wallet.

They all loved this watch the best. Every one of those grandbabies of mine cut their teeth chewing on it."

"You mean those dents were…," Alex began.

"I think it was the coldness of the metal that felt good on their little gums. Eased the pain, you know."

"And the marks on the watch were…"

"From their teeth. Every one."

Alex hung his head. "I'm so sorry…I…"

Jill tried to help. "Sir, my husband had no idea…"

"It's all right," the man whispered. He slipped the watch into his pocket. "What's done is done. I know you meant well. Just tell me what I owe you and I'll be on my way."

Alex, a worrier, lost sleep over his terrible mistake. Night after night, he lay awake and thought about how unhappy the man had looked when he saw what he had done to the watch. What made the situation so bad was that there was simply no way to make it right. No way at all.

Six months had passed when Alex looked up and was shocked to see the same customer step into his shop. He'd not expected to encounter him again—no way would the man *ever* give *him* more business. Not after what he'd done. Yet here he was. Back in the shop.

Alex tried to remain calm, but his heart began to race and he felt his face grow hot. *Was the man in to chew him out? To tell him he planned to sue? To demand restitution?* Calling on every ounce of control he had, Alex pretended to be calm. "Good morning. May I help you?"

The customer spoke as if nothing had happened. "Do you sell new watches?"

"Yes. We do." Slowed by his shaking hands, Alex unlocked the display case and got out a tray. He stood quietly while the man looked at each watch.

"Do you take trade-ins? You know, old pieces for new?"

For this man, anything. "Yes. Of course."

The man continued to look. "Your wife. Has she had the baby yet?"

"Excuse me?" Alex was so rattled he thought he'd misunderstood.

"When I was here before, I saw that she was expecting," the man said, not looking up. "Has she had the baby yet?"

"Oh, yes sir. A boy. Ten weeks old today."

"Congratulations."

"Thank you."

Back to the watches. "I like this one." He pointed to an inexpensive, everyday, stainless-steel model. "Could we talk about a trade?"

"Of course." Alex didn't care *what* it was the man had brought in—a string of fake pearls, a plastic ring from a gum machine— a pair of old glasses for that matter! He was ready to *give* the man the watch. Anything else he wanted too.

From his pocket, the man pulled out a watch. A pocket watch. *The* pocket watch.

Alex could find no words.

"Do you go to church?" the man asked.

"Yes—every Sunday," said Alex.

"And when you're there, do you hold your son in your lap?"

"Yes. I do."

"Does he have teeth yet?"

"No."

"A little young yet, I suppose, but it won't be long."

Alex searched for words. "Sir, I can't take your pocket watch in exchange for this new one. It's real gold. This one's only stainless steel. Yours is old and valuable. This one is inexpensive and new. You just take the watch. No charge. I want you to have it."

"No. I'm only interested in a trade. I'll tell you why. Soon that little baby of yours will take to fussing when you hold him in church. He'll be drooling and gnawing on his fist—needing something to cool his gums. Take this watch. Carry it in your pocket and let him chew on it next time you're in church."

"But…"

"You won't mind if it gets dented and scratched, will you?"

"No, sir. Of course not, but…"

The man smiled. "Then I want you to have it—for your son. You know—to help ease the pain."

There is a time for everything,
and a season for every activity under heaven.
ECCLESIASTES 3:1

CHAPTER NINETEEN

VANNA AND ME

Pass those down this way."

"Let me see."

"Wow! You look fabulous, Michelle."

"These turned out great!"

We were at work, but it was lunch-break time. ICU nurse Michelle was passing around prints of the photos she'd had taken at the new "glamour portrait studio" that had opened up last month in the mall.

"Your hair is gorgeous."

"And your makeup—your skin looks flawless."

"Even your teeth look whiter."

"How *do* they do that?"

"How much did it cost?"

"Are those your own clothes?"

Michelle giggled. "Black leather? A feather boa? A purple cowboy hat? What do *you* think? Of course those aren't my real clothes. They have all these outfits in the studio. You get to pick what you want to wear. There are jewelry and scarves, all kinds of accessories and stuff."

"What does your husband Rich think of the pictures?"

"He likes them."

"Uh-huh. I bet he *really* likes *this* one."

"Girl, look at you!"

Michelle blushed. In one particular photo our hardworking coworker—by day a scrub-suit-and-support-hose kind of gal—was decked out in a racy, low-cut red gown and a pair of long sparkly earrings. Not only that, but no-nonsense, "let's get down to business" Michelle had been captured on film with a pouty, painted mouth and heavy-lidded "come and get me" eyes.

"I'll be hanging that one in our bedroom."

Later that evening I was telling my friend Cheryl, who lived next door, about Michelle's pictures. "She looked really pretty. Very feminine," I said as I described the photos.

"You say she had them done at that new place in the mall? I've seen their ads in the paper. The 'before' and 'after' shots they show are amazing."

"What they did to Michelle was incredible," I agreed. "Must be special lighting or something."

"Have you ever thought about having glamour photos done?" asked Cheryl.

"Yeah, I admit I've *thought* about it. But I just don't know."

"It might be fun."

"Michelle said it was."

"Isn't your wedding anniversary next month?"

"The thirteenth."

"Mine's the twenty-first. Why don't we go do it together and surprise our husbands?"

"I don't know, Cheryl," I hedged. "I'm not so sure I'm the glamorous type. What if the whole thing feels silly? It might be a total waste of money."

"If you don't like the pictures you don't have to buy any. That's what the ad says. Come on. Let's do it. I'll make the call."

She talked me into it.

We signed up on the Buddy Plan. Sort of like Weight Watchers or the army, I guess. The next Saturday, after telling our husbands we were going to have a ladies' lunch and afterwards do a little shopping, Cheryl and I headed toward the mall.

Upon our arrival at the photo studio—a good 20 minutes before the time for our appointment—the woman in charge glanced at Cheryl and me and whisked us directly into the makeup room. "I suppose she figured from the looks of us, they'd better allow plenty of time," whispered Cheryl.

I tried not to giggle.

As an aside—just so you know—it's not like I'm unaccustomed to cosmetics. I wear lipstick, mascara, and blush even when all I'm doing is making a trek to the post office and back. I know how to tweeze my brows, and I can navigate my way around the Clinique counter as well as anyone. Still, nothing in my experience prepared me for what lay ahead—unless you count the time that I helped spackle a wall at my second cousin's best friend's new house.

"Look up," I was instructed. "Now down, please."

"Open your eyes really wide. Close them. Okay. You can open them now."

"I need you to purse your lips for me. That's right. A bit more. Good."

So many coats of cover cream and foundation were applied to my face that I feared if I smiled, the whole business might crack. Bright lipstick. Dark eye shadow. Heavy blush in a hue called "Jungle Plum." By the spoonfuls, it seemed, makeup was smeared onto my face. No wonder those women in the "after" pictures looked so good. If they had gotten the same treatment I did, not one inch of their original selves was left uncovered.

After we were deemed suitably made up, Cheryl and I were directed to move to the studio's hairstyling station. There we were given Really Big Hair. Now lest it's been forgotten, here's a quick reminder—Cheryl and I live in the Lone Star State. The Land of Big Hair. Final Net is the Official State Hair Product. Convinced that Big Hair makes us look slimmer through the hips, we gals never leave home without it.

However, even by Texas standards, what Cheryl and I got from the stylist was over the top. She must have been a native to our state because once she had finished with our locks, we had such Big Hair that we figured folks we met on the street would stare in wonder at what had happened to our hips.

Next stop on our road to glamour was Wardrobe. Cheryl and I were shown racks and racks of clothes to choose from, along with oodles of jewelry, a dozen or more hats, evening gloves, and even a selection of fake-fur stoles. "You girls take your time," we were told. "Your portrait package includes up to three changes of clothes."

Cheryl picked out what she wanted to wear with no trouble. Not me. I couldn't decide.

"How about this purple sequined top?" suggested Cheryl.

"No way. I am *not* doing cleavage."

"This cool silver boa would look great with that V-necked black dress. It's not too low-cut."

"Feathers? Me? You're kidding."

"Annette!" Cheryl complained when she saw the first outfit I picked, "What's the exact look you're going for—something suitable for a funeral or maybe a job interview? Come on. Try on something fun!"

And since when is navy blue wool not considered fun?

I finally settled on a Gibson girl–looking white lace dress, a black leather jacket over a red silk blouse, and a turquoise jumpsuit with matching headband that I thought made me look a bit like Amelia Earhart.

Finally ready, Cheryl and I moved to the actual portrait studio where we had our pictures shot. As we were directed to turn and lean, to move this way and that, to smile and to pout, we were assured by the ponytailed photographer that we both looked good.

Really good.

The truth? We believed him. And it was fun! All of it—even the makeup and the hair and the garish, costumey clothes. Having glamour pictures done was like living out a little girl's fantasy of being a model, a movie star, and Miss America—all rolled into one. For an entire afternoon Cheryl and I were made to feel glamorous and pretty—to view ourselves as a couple of vivacious vixens rather than as the pair of chronically sleep-deprived, stretch-mark-marred, 30-something wives that we were in real life.

"I'm so glad you talked me into this," I told Cheryl as we exited the mall. "It really was fun. And I can't wait to see the pictures. Do you really think they'll be any good?"

"Sure they will. Our husbands will be thrilled."

It was only as I was driving back to my home, to dinner and laundry and kids that needed baths, that I began to feel sheepish and silly about the whole thing. Catching a glimpse of my face in the rearview mirror of my car, I thought, *Oh my! I can't believe I'm wearing so much makeup. And this hair!* I reached up to smooth it down a bit, but none of it budged. I thought back over the afternoon and began to regret what I'd done. *This isn't me. What was I thinking? A glamour portrait as an anniversary present? Randy won't know what to say. What I should have gotten him was a new pair of golf shoes.*

Then I realized—*It's not too late. All I've paid for is the sitting fee. When the proofs come in,* I decided, *I won't even go look at them. I'll just tell Cheryl that I've changed my mind.*

Pulling into the driveway, around the side of the house I could see Randy and our son Russell out playing catch. *Great,* I thought. *I'll have a chance to hurry into the house, wipe this stuff off my face, and comb out my hair. He'll never know.*

I almost made it.

But not quite.

I hadn't counted on six-year-old Rachel still being in the house. As I rounded the corner, heading down the hall toward the bathroom, she stepped out of her room facing me head-on. I think that at first my own daughter wasn't sure it was me.

"Mommy!" Rachel finally exclaimed, her eyes taking my hair and my makeup all in. "You look so—so—so bea-u-ti-ful!"

"Why, thank you, sweetie." I bent to give her a kiss, but she pulled away to look at me again. "You like my new hairdo and my new makeup?"

"Oh yes, Mommy," she said with awe in her voice. "It makes you look just like Vanna."

I struggled not to smile at this, the ultimate compliment that could be bestowed on me by my little girl. No one, in her six-year-old's view, could ever epitomize glamour and beauty more than Vanna White, the lovely, evening gown–clad hostess of the nightly game show *Wheel of Fortune.* Though Rachel had no interest in the show's contestants or prizes, whenever it came on she was on her knees in front of the TV, poised to see the lovely Vanna.

After I'd sent Rachel out to play, I locked myself in the bathroom and studied my reflection in the mirror that hung over the sink. *Beautiful? Me?* Was a six-year-old to be believed?

She was.

At least according to my husband when, on our anniversary, he unwrapped a nicely matted and framed color eight-by-ten.

> *Your beauty should not come from outward adornment,*
> *such as braided hair*
> *and the wearing of gold jewelry and fine clothes.*
> *Instead, it should be that of your inner self,*
> *the unfading beauty of a gentle and quiet spirit,*
> *which is of great worth in God's sight.*
>
> 1 PETER 3:3-4

CHAPTER TWENTY

SWEET BABY JANE

It became every family member's personal goal to extract a smile from our adorable, newly arrived, eight-month-old foster baby, Jane.

Ten-year-old Russell squatted in front of her on the living-room floor, waved his arms, quacked like a duck, made funny faces and all kinds of silly boy sounds.

Jane stared straight ahead.

Five-year-old Rachel played peep-eye and danced her Barbie dolls across the tray of Jane's high chair.

The baby's solemn gaze did not change.

Randy held Jane in his lap and gently tickled her soft feet. He told her about the little piggy that went to market and the one that stayed home.

She didn't respond.

When I gave Jane her bath, I blew soapsud bubbles and sang about a dog named Bingo, and a spider and a waterspout.

My best efforts failed to produce even one small grin.

"She misses her mom," explained Jane's caseworker when I called her up. "Is she crying a lot?"

"No. Not much at all. She whimpers and fusses a little, but mostly stays really quiet. And another thing. I know that she *can* pull up and crawl, but she doesn't. She's not moving around or trying to explore. Wherever I put her, that's where she stays.

Nothing interests her—not even toys. Has she had her hearing checked?"

"Yes. It's just fine. Her physical exam showed her to be healthy. Annette, it sound's like she's grieving."

"You mean a baby this young *grieves?*" I'd had no idea. Yet Jane's subdued behavior *was* similar to that of an adult who was really, really sad.

"Absolutely. Give her some time. A few days. Once she's more accustomed to all of you, she'll relax, feel better, and warm up."

"And in the meantime—what should I do?"

"Annette, you *know* what to do. Just love her and care for her like she was your own."

And so I did. I fed Jane, changed her, bathed and dressed her. I put ribbons in her hair, took her on stroller rides, and read *Goodnight Moon* to her. After all, babies need cleaning and feeding, fresh air, and such. But what *this* baby needed, I discovered on the day after she arrived, was *rocking.* Only during the moments when I held her in my arms, seated in the bentwood rocking chair that Randy gave me before the birth of our first child, did Jane behave like a "normal" baby. When we rocked, she cuddled up, buried her face in my neck, and molded her little body to match the shape of mine.

So what did I do?

I rocked her. And rocked her. And rocked her some more. In the mornings, after lunch, in the afternoons, the evenings, and at night before bed, baby Jane and I rocked. I let my housework go, and I watched as the laundry piled up. I delighted Russell and Rachel by agreeing to pizza for many nights' suppers. Back and forth, back and forth.

Jane and I must have rocked to Canada and back. Three times. But despite all that rocking, contrary to her caseworker's prediction, it took more than a few days for Jane to settle in.

A week passed.

She did not smile.

Two weeks.

Still no smile.

Finally, one morning after we'd had Jane for more than two months, I went in to get her up out of her crib. When she saw me open the door, her fresh-from-sleep, glad-to-see-you little face sported a tiny grin. That afternoon, when Russell and Rachel arrived home from school, they spotted a real smile. Randy was sure that he too saw one when he put her to bed. Perhaps, as we discussed after she was asleep in her crib, Jane was feeling better about all of us. Maybe she wasn't so sad anymore.

Sure enough. After two months, though I don't know how or why, the five of us—our family and Jane—had crossed over some unseen bridge. By the end of the week Jane was smiling every day, even laughing and giggling a bit.

We all felt like we'd accomplished something big.

Before we got Jane, back when Randy and I were in training to be foster parents, it was explained to us that successful foster-care placements most often end with the child being reunited with his or her birth family. We were told that we must be diligent to never forget this fact. And no matter what the situation, it was essential that we, as foster parents, never view the birth parent as an enemy or adversary.

That particular instruction sounded good and made sense, but putting it into practice in our hearts proved difficult. As was agreed upon at the time of her placement in foster care, Jane had weekly visits with her mother. Before each meeting—which took place at the agency and lasted two hours—I bathed Jane, brushed her hair, and dressed her in something pretty.

Sometimes Jane's mother showed up. Sometimes she didn't. When she didn't make the visit there was always a good reason— car trouble, the flu, an alarm clock that didn't go off. We would wait and wait, Jane, her caseworker, and I. We would look at our watches, attempt some nonchalant chat, then look at our watches again. Sometimes Jane's mother would call; sometimes she wouldn't.

When Jane's mom did make the visits, without fail she had something critical to say to me about the way I was caring for her little girl. Jane looked thin. Was I feeding her enough meat? Jane's hair was parted on the wrong side. It looked funny pulled back like that. Jane needed new shoes. Her toes were scrunched up. The ones she was wearing were way too small.

Each time Jane's mother made such comments, though I seethed inside, I smiled, nodded acknowledgment of her observations, and held it all inside. *She's not the enemy. She's not the enemy,* I repeated to myself. *She just misses her little girl.*

During the years that our family kept foster children, curious people asked the same questions about each one: *Why was this child in our care? What was the situation with this particular little one?*

Jane was placed with us because her mother had voluntarily, temporarily, surrendered her to foster care. As far as anyone knew, there had been no abuse. Rather, Jane's mother, unmarried, uneducated, and poor, had shown up on the doorstep of a Christian foster-care and adoption agency seeking help. She needed someone to care for her child while she took some time to get on her feet, find a new job, and secure a better place to live.

For how long?

A couple of weeks, we were told by Jane's caseworker. Maybe a month. Three months, tops.

It was during the time we cared for Jane that we learned of this caseworker trait: With even the most well-meaning of them (just like with God!) a day is as a thousand years, a thousand years as a day. Over and over, we were told that Jane would be leaving our home in a few days. Each time, as best we could, we steeled ourselves for the difficult goodbye. In preparation, I would wash all of Jane's clothes and gather her scattered things from all over the house—doing my best to keep my chin up and stay convinced that Jane's leaving was the best thing for all.

You can do this, I would tell myself. *It's going to be hard, but you can do it. Jane needs to be with her mother and her brother and sister. Reunification is what foster parenting is all about. This is a good thing.*

But over and over, after we had done our best to get prepared, Jane's leaving would be delayed. Each time, it was because yet a new problem had surfaced in her mother's life.

It was difficult not to imagine that baby Jane would be with us forever.

Early on a Friday morning five months after Jane had come to stay with us, her social worker called to tell me that in preparation for her return home, Jane would be going to her mother's for a weekend visit. Things were looking up. Jane's mom had a new apartment and a new job. She was excited and planned to take Jane to the zoo and to the park. It would be good for the two of them to have sort of a trial run before Jane went back home for good. Someone from the agency would stop by and pick her up and take her on the 30-mile car trip to her mom's new place. This was short notice, but could I get Jane ready and pack her a bag?

Certainly. Actually, a little break would be nice. Being without Jane for the weekend would also help us prepare for when she was really gone—which from the looks of things was going to be soon.

I stood in the driveway and watched the caseworker's car disappear from sight, swallowed a lump in my throat, then went back into the house, poured myself a cup of coffee, and sat down to read the morning paper—a ritual I'd enjoyed before Jane came. Without her chattering, the house was quiet, so I turned on the TV to have some noise. *How quickly I've become accustomed to having a little one in the house,* I mused. *What did I do with my time before Jane?*

I cooked and cleaned—that's what!

This would be a great day to get caught up. I started a load of laundry, mopped the kitchen floor, and stripped all the beds. I dusted, scrubbed the bathrooms, and vacuumed all the carpets. Before time for Russell and Rachel to return home from school, I made a trip to the grocery store. I'd make their favorite meal tonight—one with more than two food items on each plate!

We were eating dinner when the police officer's call came. Jane's mother had been arrested. They were unable to reach anyone from the agency. Could we come pick the baby up?

Before we'd swallowed our bites, we'd bolted out the door.

At the city jail, Randy stayed with Russell and Rachel in the lobby while I was led back to a cell. Jane was asleep in her mother's arms. "I haven't done anything wrong." Her words tumbled out. "I swear. Not in a long time. The police—they picked me up on an old warrant."

I didn't know what to say.

"Jane's things. You'll need them. Can you go get them? They're at my apartment. It's unlocked."

I took sleeping Jane from her arms and told her we would.

Jane's mom spent only a couple of days in jail. The charges against her were not deemed serious, and someone came and paid her fine. Three months after the arrest, Jane went back to live with her mother for good. We have not seen her since.

Losing Jane was hard. I wondered then and I wonder still what went through her little baby mind.

Did she wonder what happened to us?

Did she feel abandoned?

Did she grieve?

My prayer is that Jane didn't lose her smile.

I will not forget you!
ISAIAH 49:15

CHAPTER TWENTY-ONE

LEXIE'S LOST CHILDREN

There could be no mistake. All the signs were present. Lexie, never married, not too bright, and the mother of several offspring already, was pregnant again. Out of our children's earshot, husband Randy and I discussed her unfortunate fertile state of affairs.

"You'd think she'd learn!" I shook my head.

"Remember last time? Lexie's not exactly what you'd call a good mother," my husband replied.

"I don't think she knows any better," I said. "Looking back, I should have forced her to get into the car with me so I could take her in to see Dr. Ross. I should have paid no attention to her howls. But it's too late now."

"You're right. It would be out of the question to do—you know—anything *now*." Randy sighed. "If this time turns out to be anything like her last pregnancy, from now until the day she delivers she'll do nothing but lie around—"

"—and complain about the food," I finished. "I'll take care of her this time. I'll see that she has whatever she needs, but"—I meant what I said—"never again. Soon as we can, we're getting this problem taken care of once and for all."

Over the next few weeks, Randy and the children and I watched Lexie—our sweet, dumb little Siamese cat—get fatter and fatter and fatter. She was pregnant all right, getting rounder every day.

As her time drew near, so big was her middle, so uncomfortable was she, that every time one of us tried to pick her up, Lexie, who normally loved to be held, hissed at us and threatened to scratch. Except for regular trips outside (we are a house without a litter box), the mother-to-be did little besides eat and sleep.

One day, I let Lexie out just before time to leave for work. I watched as she waddled around to her favorite spot on the side of the house. I planned to wait, then let her back in, but suddenly I remembered that I'd left the iron on. I dashed back inside to turn it off. When I came back out, she was gone. I called and called, but she didn't come. Concerned, but running too late to do much of a search, I cracked open the door to the garage, got into my car, and drove away, confident that if today was the day that Lexie was to deliver, she could do so in the warmth and safety of the garage.

Hours later, when I arrived home, Lexie met me on the doorstep. She was weary-looking, rail-thin, and ravenously hungry. Evidently, today *had* been her big day.

"Look at you! All slim and trim. Where are your babies?" I asked as I dug for my house key. "You had them today, didn't you!" She rubbed, impatient, against my leg. "Are they in the garage? Did you have them out there?" Once inside I poured her some food and rushed to the garage for a look.

I couldn't find the kittens. They weren't anywhere in the garage. I looked in every box, up on every shelf, in every corner. They weren't there.

Lexie, instead of acting frantic like most separated-from-their-babies new mothers would, appeared relaxed and unconcerned.

I went outside and walked the perimeter of our house, checking behind every bush. Still no baby kittens.

Lexie seemed not to mind.

When Russell and Rachel came home from school, we looked up and down the neighborhood to no avail.

Lexie yawned and stretched, meowed for fresh food, and chose not to participate in the search.

Three days passed. We gave up. Then the phone rang.

"Annette?" It was Eva, our next-door neighbor. "Did your cat have kittens?"

"Yes, but we think they died. She came home without them. We searched the neighborhood, but never did find them."

"I did. They're in my storage building."

"You're kidding! Are they alive?"

"Yes, but cold and starving. They're bawling their little heads off."

"I'll be right there."

It was unbelievable. No nourishment for days, and all three of the kittens were still alive. Turns out, Eva had propped the door of her little-used storage building open three mornings ago to let it air out. That same afternoon, she had closed the building back up, and it had remained locked ever since. Best we could figure out, on that day Lexie had slipped inside the storage building unseen by anyone and given birth. Likely, it was while she was gone for food or water that Eva had shut the door, leaving her outside the building, the kittens inside.

I scooped up the pitiful animals—little more than bones and matted fur—and rushed them home. "Lexie," I called, "come see what I've found." Wouldn't she be thrilled! I placed a soft towel in a plastic laundry basket and put the kittens inside.

Hearing my voice and assuming it was time for dinner, the little mother first scampered toward me but then flattened her ears and skidded to a stop.

"Your babies," I said.

Lexie was *not* thrilled. She arched her back, got a wild-eyed look in her eyes, and hissed.

"Don't be so silly," I chided. "You need to feed your babies. They're cold. They're hungry. Say hello to your children." I lifted her into the basket.

She jumped out.

I put her back in.

She jumped out again.

I chased her from behind the couch, through the kitchen, and finally pulled her out from under our bed. This time, when I put her back into the basket I covered the top so she couldn't get out.

What a terrible scene. She howled and tried to claw her way out. The kittens, starving and sensing the proximity of milk, frantically tried to get at her.

She fought to get away.

What to do?

I called the vet.

"After being separated for so long," Dr. Ross said, "she's forgotten the kittens are hers. She may refuse to nurse them. If so, you'll have to feed them with a bottle. But don't give up yet. Keep her closed up with them in a quiet place for the next few hours. She may take to them still."

I followed his advice and closed the four of them in the utility room, with food and water nearby.

One hour passed before I peeked in. No bonding yet. Lexie wasn't letting the kittens get near her. They, climbing over each other in panicked attempts to appease their hunger, were mewing bloody murder. I closed the door.

Two hours—Lexie wasn't looking at the kittens, but was no longer trying to scramble away.

Three hours, and she was letting the exhausted kittens get close, though refusing to lie down so they could nurse.

Four hours? *Eureka!* Milk at last! I looked in to see Lexie stretched out, the noses of the kittens buried in her side.

By the next morning you would have never known that the little family had ever been apart. Lexie was purring. The kittens were sleeping. Everyone was happy. But I was not taking any chances. In case Lexie decided to make a run for it, I bought a litter box. The family could stay inside.

It was not over yet. That night, Randy and I experienced the oddest of awakenings from our sound sleep. First I felt Lexie jump up on the foot of our bed. She liked to snooze against my warm back—but tonight she should have been in the basket with her kittens. What was she doing away from them now? She gingerly padded her way toward our heads.

Then I heard the mew.

What?

No!

A kitten. *Her* kitten. Lexie had hauled the little thing in her mouth, clear across the house, in order to deposit him on the pillow between Randy's head and mine. For safekeeping, we could only assume. Awake now, and incredulous at what she'd done, we lay there, cradling the kitten to see what she would do next.

In a minute, up she hopped with another kitten. Soon the third one too. So, did Lexie then, as Randy and I expected, curl up with her family in our warm bed? No. She did not. She jumped down and was gone in the dark. We waited. Waited some more. After ten minutes, I got up, put the kittens back into their basket, and went in search of their mother.

I found her enjoying her beauty sleep all alone, curled up on the end of the couch, confident that Randy and I would take care of her brood. When I called her name, she lazily raised her head and voiced a soft meow. *I've fed them,* she seemed to say. *I'm tired. Can't you watch them for a while?*

My two children are almost grown. One is out of the house, away at college, and the other is not far behind.

When I'm at church, the market, or at the mall, often I observe young mothers with their little ones in tow. I think they are darling and sweet, but honestly, I don't feel even a twinge of desire for another baby of my own—though I think some grandchildren one day would be nice.

Raising children, especially babies, is difficult. When I remember the years that I had little babies, I recall a series of magical moments strung together in one long sleep-deprived blur. Like many young women, back then I was unsure and ill at ease and yet so determined to be a good mother that I found it difficult to accept help, even when it was generously offered. During those long years, what I wouldn't have given for one long night of uninterrupted sleep.

Perhaps Lexie wasn't so dumb after all.

> *Can a mother forget the baby at her breast*
> *and have no compassion on the child she has borne?*
> *Though she may forget,*
> *I will not forget you!*
> ISAIAH 49:15

CLOCKING IN
PART FOUR

CHAPTER TWENTY-TWO

NO FEAR

I know few women who manage to keep up with their ironing. Gone are the days when housewives enjoyed the luxury of devoting entire mornings to getting the laundry all done up at once. Most wives and moms, like me, press their families' clothing on a daily as-needed-to-be-worn schedule.

Everyone's got their own system of dealing with the family's stash of clean-but-unironed clothes. Some of us go right ahead and hang up everything that's clean—wrinkles and all. Others pile the wadded-up duds in a big basket that's kept on the floor of the closet at the end of the hall.

Dig. Pluck. Press. That's my family's morning routine.

So what was I, on a Tuesday morning last winter, doing standing at the ironing board pressing two—count them—*two* white dress shirts for my husband (who's a coach and wears athletic attire to work every day) when Sunday church was five days away?

Did he have an out-of-town job interview?

No.

A banquet or a wedding to attend?

No again.

So what then?

I was leaving town. On a plane. To serve on a medical mission trip deep in the heart of Mexico. Though I've set foot on three continents so far, I'm always a bit anxious when I travel—more so when I leave my family behind. It is part of my normal routine, each time that I go, to scurry around at the last minute so I can leave my house clean and my laundry caught up. All that cleaning and scrubbing, washing and folding makes me feel better.

But not this time. After serving on more than 20 mission trips—traveling to Mexico, Central America, and even Africa—for the first time the thought crossed my mind that I might not make it back home. No matter how much I prayed, talked sternly to myself, and reviewed the facts, I was unable to shake a growing sense of unease.

I'd been making mission trips for a dozen years, and not once had anything bad happened.

Yet I still felt afraid.

Insomnia brings with it crazy thoughts. Lying in bed two nights before I was to leave, it came to me that my husband should have, ready in his closet, two clean and pressed shirts and two pairs of dark slacks. Should my anxious musings come true and I meet an out-of-the-country demise, he would need two freshly pressed shirts, one to wear to *visitation* (that's what folks around here call the evening set aside for neighbors and friends to view the dead and to visit with the family at the funeral home) and one to wear to my funeral.

Couldn't I bank on the expectation that under such circumstances Randy would iron a shirt for himself? Not a chance. Wrinkles have never bothered the man one whit. Faced with a wadded 100-percent-cotton button-down, I knew exactly what he would do. He'd pop it in the dryer, spin it on *hot* for ten minutes, take it out, put it on, and assume he looked *good*.

What would people think?

No. I needed to iron him some shirts.

Given my concern about the trip, and acknowledging my growing anxiety, did I consider canceling, staying home? I wanted to, but no. Actually I found it embarrassing that I, an experienced traveler, was capable of having such overwrought thoughts. My fears, even to me, seemed silly and melodramatic. After all, plans were in place. An expensive airline ticket had been bought. Dear south-of-the-border friends were expecting me and the rest of the team.

It would have been inconsiderate and irresponsible to back out, for this trip was a carefully coordinated Mexican–American effort, a year in the making. While generous Americans provided the several thousand dollars of funding, Mexican ministers, doctors, and dentists did all the preparation and would direct the week's work. They had made all the plans and arrangements. Our Mexican Christian family members were expecting us, counting on us, counting on *me* to come and help out.

But here's the truth. While I spent weeks fussing at myself for letting my imagination get the best of me, actually the qualms I felt about my upcoming trip were rooted in reality. This mission trip *was* a bit different from any I'd yet been on.

First off, because of work schedules and other prior commitments, no men were going. Some had planned to make the trip, but at the last minute had been forced to cancel. This time, traveling to Mexico along with me were just Irene, who was a physician; Laura, a young nursing student; pharmacy worker Toni; and the children's Bible teacher, Marolyn—five women in all. Lest I make this arrangement sound worse than it was, we did know that once we arrived in Mexico, we gals would be in good hands. The group of us would be met at the airport by Mexican families who would care for us and watch out for us like we were blood kin.

But still—during our travels to and from, we would have felt better had one of our husbands or Christian brothers been along.

Then there was the week's actual work plan. Instead of setting up our mobile free medical clinics in tiny rural villages and towns like we'd done in times past, on this trip we would spend our week holding clinic inside the walls of a Mexican prison.

I'd never been in a prison. Ever. Not in the U.S., and certainly not in Mexico. I imagined that the place would be dark and dank, dirty, and likely infested with insects and rats. As for working with the prisoners—what would they be like? Dark, dank, and dirty too? Would we five women be safe?

It was all set up when we arrived.

Manuel was the preacher in the place where we went. We ate at his house. Some of the Mexican team members slept there. Now married and the father of two darling children, Manuel had once been a prisoner himself. Devoted to God and committed to spreading the good news of Christ, Manuel had a great love for and a great calling to minister to those who lived behind bars. Several times a week he rode the bus there to teach, to preach, to offer encouragement, and to share hope.

Prison ministry was obviously Manuel's gift. While we sat around his table on the night of our arrival, sipping *café con leche* and nibbling on *pan dulce,* he excitedly told us about his work, described his successes, shared the challenges he faced, answered our questions, and told us about his future plans.

There were about 300 prisoners held in the facility where he worked, he explained, mostly men, but a few mothers and children.

Women? Children? In the same facility? I'd had no idea.

Did they have access to medical care? Did they have medicine? First-aid supplies?

No. Not unless their individual families brought it to them. Not even aspirins or bandages. Many of the prisoners to whom Manuel ministered complained of illnesses both serious and mild. Like folks on the outside, they suffered from a variety of aches and pains, from rashes and headaches, and intestinal upsets. Many had bad teeth that caused them great pain.

What about food?

Now of *that* they had plenty. Adequate shelter too. In actuality, this prison, run by a man Manuel deemed *good,* was one of the better in Mexico. Cruelty by the guards was not tolerated. Classes were offered to those who wanted to learn a trade or a skill. Seldom did fights or violence break out. As far as prisons went, it was likely one of the best.

Manuel smiled, stretched, and yawned. "Sisters, tomorrow you will see for yourselves."

The next morning we five American women arrived on the prison grounds and were joined by Manuel and a half-dozen Mexican men—student preachers, their instructor, two doctors, and a dentist. Before being allowed admittance, all of us were required to show our paperwork and passports, sign in, and present our bags to be checked. After that we were directed one by one into a damp, closet-sized room where we were frisked from head to toe by a female attendant.

Finally we were directed down a hall, through several double-locked doors, outside, down a walk, and through a final locked gate to the inside.

Unlike the dark dungeon I'd imagined, what we saw first was a tidy though trampled shady grass courtyard about half the size of a football field. Utilitarian cinder-block living quarters, classrooms, workshops, shower rooms, and a dining hall opened onto the courtyard.

It didn't look so bad. Except for the tall surrounding walls, topped with barbed wire and patrolled by nimble-footed armed guards, the place could have passed for a school or government facility.

The day was sunny and pleasant. Under peaceful groves of orange trees, a few dozen men dressed in street clothes roamed about freely like folks would in a park. Some sat on benches. Others leaned against the sides of buildings. One man swept a sidewalk. Another squatted over a water faucet, scrubbing pots and pans. Yet another was hanging out some clothes. Several men were busy weaving colorful hammocks, their work suspended from the branches of trees. Others bent low as they carved artistic shapes from pieces of wood.

Carving tools? Inside a prison?

"Yes," said a guard nonchalantly. "It is no problem. They are allowed to sell the things they make to us guards and to visitors. Maybe at the end of the day you will want to buy something."

Wide-eyed, we took it all in.

As the group of us was led by Manuel, single-file, in the direction of the classroom where we would be holding our clinic, I heard the high-pitched voices of small children. I looked around, but could not determine where the sound was coming from. No children were in sight. It was only when Manuel veered off course toward a space in the wall that I spotted a half-dozen little faces pressed against the slats of a tall gate—the partition separating the male section of the prison from the smaller area that held the women and their children. "Manuel! Manuel!" the children chirped when they spotted their friend. I saw tiny brown hands reach through the slats. The sight and sound of them reminded me of tiny birds calling from their nests.

"¡Hola, niños—hola!" He walked over and greeted them, touched their little hands. "¿Cómo está?"

At the sight of children just like mine being raised behind bars, tears filled my eyes, and I had to turn my head.

After conversing only a few moments with the little ones, Manuel led us on, explaining that we would see that section of the prison later. Once all of the men had consulted with the doctors and dentist, the room would be cleared out, and the women and children would be brought in.

When we reached the place where we would hold clinic, comfortably shielded from the eyes that had so carefully scrutinized us as we walked through the prison yard, we team members began to set up. Each of us a veteran of many trips, we all knew just what to do to transform the shabby room into an efficient clinic. First we cordoned off physician consultation areas, each with two chairs and a small table in between. Next we claimed the spot with the most light—near the window—for the dentist to work. Two of us dragged a larger table to his area since he would need space for his instruments, disinfecting solutions, towels, and such. The pharmacy area required lots of table space since the free medications the doctors would dispense needed to be arranged in alphabetical order. Finally, a chair was set up just inside the classroom door. That is where I would take the inmates' blood pressure.

In efficient North American style, we had the place set up lickety-split. Okay now—we were ready for patients. Time to start—right? (The sooner we get started, the sooner we finish, was the thought that I kept to myself.)

Not yet, we were told by Manuel. First there was to be some preaching, a prayer, and an explanation of why we had come. That was good. After all, we had traveled to Mexico not only to minister to sick bodies, but also to sick souls.

So.

Was there a prison chapel? A meeting hall? Some other place where the service would be held?

Manuel didn't answer, instead motioned that we follow him.

When the five of us, followed by the Mexican team members, stepped out from the dim classroom-turned-clinic into the bright sunlight, it took a few seconds for our eyes to adjust. I wished for the sunglasses that I'd been told I couldn't bring in. When we finally could see, we all noted that there were no men hanging around outside like there had been when we first arrived. We wondered to each other where they had gone. Was it work time? Late breakfast time? Where was everybody?

Then we saw them. Three hundred dark-skinned men, standing four and five deep in a huge, inward-facing circle in the unshaded center of the prison yard. When we approached, the circle parted, and we five, along with the Mexican team members, were directed to stand dead center inside.

Now I've been the focus of attention many times in my life. Over and over I've been called to take the platform so that I could speak before large groups. Standing before crowds does not generally give me the willies. Oh, but *this* time it did! Never, ever in my life had I faced a situation remotely *anything* like this surreal scene. In front of us, behind us, and on both sides, we were surrounded by Mexican prisoners, all of them staring, most with their feet planted and their arms folded across their chests.

Willing ourselves invisible, we five women looked at our feet, stood with our shoulders hunched, and wished the event to be over soon. *Please!* Really soon.

Then Manuel began to speak and the men changed. I watched their faces soften and their arms drop to their sides. He talked about Jesus. About how people inside and outside prisons live in bondage to sin. He spoke of God's saving grace and how He alone could set captive hearts free. The men, captivated by Manuel's booming yet gentle voice, stood knee-locked still and drank in every word he said. When someone led a prayer, they bowed their heads. When we sang hymns, some of them wiped at their eyes.

As I look back on the week that I spent in a Mexican prison, a variety of scenes come to mind. Smells, for one, trigger vivid memories. Since my return, every time I walk down the personal-care aisle at the grocery store, I'm taken back to the prison. I recall how, when the men rolled up their sleeves for me to take their blood pressure, the strong scent of soap wafted up from their just-scrubbed skin. Not a single man smelled bad.

I remember the taste of fresh-squeezed orange juice. One gentleman, once he'd seen the doctor, ran out into the courtyard and began rapidly plucking fruit from a tree. Using six oranges for each, one by one he hand-squeezed glasses of juice for all of us. It was the best I have ever tasted.

When I think back, I can picture the face of one man who, after living in prison for seven years, was about to be freed. Manuel had led him to Christ. All week long he worked by Manuel's side, tirelessly writing down names, scouting the yard for the person whose next turn it was to be seen, moving tables and fetching more chairs. He planned to go to preacher training school as soon as he got out of prison.

I'm going back to the prison this year. Plans are already in the works. Manuel reports that our week of service prepared the soil for the planting of many seeds. He's been busy harvesting ever since.

Though this trip I'll be much less afraid, it's unlikely I'll forgo my regular pre-trip cleaning spree. As always, prior to departure, I'll stay up late scrubbing and wiping, polishing and shining. Lack of faith, one might suggest? Disbelief in God's providential care?

Of course not! Need proof? I've got it right here. This year, I'm leaving my husband's shirts right where they are—wadded up in the big to-be-ironed basket of clothes.

> *Set me free from my prison,*
> *that I may praise your name.*
> *Then the righteous will gather about me*
> *because of your goodness to me.*
> PSALM 142:7

CHAPTER TWENTY-THREE

HAVING THE LAST WORD

It all started when Minnie Lee Trevor donated money to the church with the stipulation that it be used to purchase new miniblinds to hang in all of the Sunday-school rooms. A woman sensitive to appearance, she was tired of seeing the ragged way the windows looked from the outside when she drove by on the way to visit her sister at the rest home.

Miss Minnie's donation was a generous one, and the entire congregation was grateful except for one thing. While the miniblinds looked oh-so-much-better than the musty, frayed, 20-year-old drapes they replaced, their installation had the effect of making the rest of the rooms look shabby by contrast.

Everyone agreed that something needed to be done.

Before the start of their monthly Monday business meeting, the four deacons of the church made a slow walk-through of the empty education hall to see exactly what they were up against. "Carpet," observed Roy Safford, rubbing the toe of his boot against a bald spot worn nearly right through. "We need to replace this carpet."

"Paint too. How many years you reckon it's been since these walls had a fresh coat?" asked Al Beard.

"Too many. That's for sure," said Samuel Keys. "To tell you the truth, I don't believe they've been painted since this building was built. What's that been—27 years?"

"It's gonna cost us."

"Got that right."

"Boys," Ben Bates directed the group, "we'd best get down to business and take a look at the books."

While finding money for the sprucing-up presented a challenge to the congregation's skimpy budget, that was nothing compared to getting the ladies of the church to agree on what color to paint the rooms and what kind of carpet to lay down. Knowing better than to trust such important decisions to the men of the church, once they knew that the work had been approved, the deacons' wives wasted no time in forming a decorating committee.

Samuel's wife, Lucille, led the crusade for butter yellow walls and royal blue Berber. (No one was surprised. Everyone knew that Lucille Keys had a liberal lean.)

Ben Bates's wife, Ellen, and her sisters, Maggie and Lynn, believed that bright white and elegant bronze plush was the only way to go.

Al Beard's wife, Aleen, kept reminding the other woman of her degree in Early Childhood Development (as if she'd ever given them a chance to forget). She was of the expert opinion that soft blue walls combined with muted gray carpet would help the children learn their Bible verses better.

Wisely, the deacons went with the inspired selections of light beige and dark beige. "We got a good deal—practically wholesale" was what they agreed to tell their wives.

On the first Sunday that the work was all done, the deacons' wives served celebration coffee and doughnuts, and everyone agreed that the education hall looked really nice. Bright. Light. Clean. Which explained why, of course, now something *had* to be done about the sanctuary.

"Here we go again," said Samuel at the next meeting.

"Carpet?" asked Roy.

"Paint?" asked Al.

"We gonna do the outside while we're at it or just the inside?"

"Inside for now," said Ben.

"If we do the paintin' ourselves, it won't cost as much."

"The way the budget looks, this time we'll have to."

"When we gonna do it?"

They started two Saturdays later. Armed with drop cloths, rollers, brushes, and buckets, the deacons of the church set to work at seven o'clock sharp. They started at the front, first putting a fresh coat on the walls around the baptistery, and worked out sideways from there. Because of all the trim work around the pulpit area, the front was all that they had completed by the time Roy's wife showed up at noon with steak finger baskets from Dairy Queen.

"Looks good. Real good," Roy's wife assured them. "You fellows keep up the good work. Now that the hard part's done I bet the rest will go faster. I'll be back this afternoon to bring y'all some cold drinks."

They took their food outside. It felt good to sit down on the back steps of the church, breathe some fresh air, and rest while they ate. Al, who'd been a deacon for less than a year, chewed on a french fry, mulling a question in his mind until he got up the nerve to ask it of the others. "I heard something the other day about there nearly being a split in this church a long time ago. Seems hard to believe. Any of you around back then?"

"I was," said Ben. "Samuel, you were too."

"Me too," said Roy. "Was it ever a mess."

"There's no mess like a church mess. What was it over?" asked Al.

"Beer."

"Nah. In the church? You're kidding me!"

"He's right," said Roy. "Nearly had a split over Pabst Blue Ribbon Beer."

Samuel told the tale. "When this church started, we didn't have anything but a tiny little run-down frame building to meet in. I remember helping my daddy and some of the other men work to fix it up. Back then they did with what they had. As the church roll grew and more people started to come, they knocked out one of the side walls to add some more room. That helped, but before long, the new part was full too. This church was literally bursting at the seams."

"That was right about the time when Miss Effie died," said Ben.

"She was a good woman. God rest her soul," said Roy.

"That she was. No telling how many motherless kids she helped raise—including her nephew, Thomas Mitchell."

"I've heard of him," said Al.

"Used to be a big landowner around here. Anyway, when his Aunt Effie passed away, Thomas was just all tore up. Aunt Effie had meant the world to him growing up. So he decided, in memory of her, to donate some money to the church," said Samuel.

"Lots of money," said Ben.

"A *ton* of money." Roy whistled. "Enough money to build a brand-new, big, nice church building to replace the old one that was here."

"That sounds mighty nice," said Al.

"Not everybody in the church thought so. Problem was, Thomas Mitchell was not a churchgoing man. Did not have the best of reputations. Fact was, he made all his money selling Pabst beer."

"Owned one of the biggest distribution plants in the state," said Roy.

"And there were a lot of church members who did not take kindly to the idea of beer money being used to build a new church."

"I can see their point," said Al.

"Some folks said that the Lord could use beer money same as he could use farm money," said Ben. "They thought that not only should the church take the money, they should be so grateful as to put Thomas Mitchell's name on a big sign in the yard."

"But other people said they would leave and never come back if the church took the money," said Roy. "This went on for months before they finally decided what to do."

"What *did* they do?" asked Al.

"Well, after meeting on it and studying on it, praying on it too, I guess, the leaders of the church told Thomas Mitchell that he could give the money as long as he understood that his name stayed out of it. There would be no mention of his name in the paper. His name wouldn't go on the cornerstone, and it wouldn't show up on the deed. They would take the money so long as it was as if he didn't have anything to do with the new building at all."

"That's enough to make a fellow mad," said Al.

"You'd think so, but Thomas said that was no problem to him. He'd said all along that he was giving the money not for himself, but for his Aunt Effie."

"And so that's how we came to have this here building that we're painting today," finished Samuel.

"It's been a good one," said Ben.

"Served the Lord well," added Roy, "all thanks to Thomas Mitchell."

"Whatever happened to the man?" asked Al.

"You won't believe. Less than five years after he gave the money to the church, he turned his life over to the Lord, sold his beer plant, and started coming to church as faithful as his Aunt Effie. Rarely have I seen such change take place in a man's life. He lives out of state now, but occasionally he visits, usually around Christmastime. He'll slip in and set himself on a back pew. Good a man as you could meet. Likely you've seen him, Al, but you just didn't know who he was."

Story told, Samuel stood up and stretched. "Ready, boys? We've set long enough. Best get back to work."

Roy's wife's prediction was right. The sides of the sanctuary went much faster than the front. The four of them worked out a system of who did what, and by midafternoon, all the deacons lacked was the back wall and the foyer. They agreed between them that the rest rooms and the cry room could wait until next week.

It was Al who, in preparation for painting the back wall, reached way up and took down the church clock. So dusty was the top of the thing that it was obvious it had never been moved. When Al turned the clock over to wipe off the back, his mouth fell wide open. So great was his shock that he could barely talk. "You guys better come quick!" he finally got out.

Roy saw it first. "Would you look at that!"

Then Ben. "You mean that all these years…"

Finally Samuel. "All this time…"

"If that don't beat all!"

"What do you think we should do?" asked Al.

"I don't know," Ben scratched his head.

"I'm not sure," Roy said.

"Men, I say we paint the wall and just hang her back up," Samuel decided.

"I agree."

"Me too."

And with reverence and care, that's exactly what they did.

For 27 years Thomas Mitchell had kept true to his word. Not even once had his name been written in the newspaper in connection with his gift. Nowhere on the church deed had it ever appeared.

Hearing the story, even a person as conservative as I voices regret that Thomas Mitchell, who by all accounts turned out to be a very good, honest, and moral man, never got even a bit of credit for such a generous deed.

Not to worry, such a person is told with a wink.

To this day, in the back of that church hangs a special clock. Printed on the back side? Pabst Blue Ribbon Beer.

*A gift opens the way for the giver
and ushers him into the presence of the great.*
PROVERBS 18:16

CHAPTER TWENTY-FOUR

ON A WING
AND A PRAYER

Should we try to catch an earlier flight?"

"Why not?"

"Worth a try."

I, first in line, am elected to ask. "Three of us are traveling together. Our next flight leaves in four hours. Could we, by chance, get an earlier connection to Dallas?"

I watch—with hope but little confidence—as the ticket agent punches her keyboard. She punches and punches, then punches some more. Finally: "Three?" she asks.

"Yes." My bag has grown heavy in my arms.

"I have seats available on a flight boarding for Dallas in ten minutes. All are in the back of the plane. Is that a problem?"

"No, not at all. We'll take them." I turn to the others and flash a jubilant thumbs-up. The three of us are shortly to be on our way home.

Home.

We've been gone more than a week, my mother, my friend Toni, and I—to Veracruz, Mexico, on a medical mission trip. A dozen years before, when we made the first of many of these trips, it was with the knowledge that we had been richly blessed. We traveled with a deep desire in our hearts to share what we had and to serve the poor. But what amazed us on that first trip, and what surprises us each time we go, is how we are blessed, touched, and loved by those we set out to serve.

The three of us sit quietly now, buckled side by side, waiting for takeoff. Not one of us speaks. Just hours ago, in the rainy predawn darkness, we lay side by side in sleeping bags on a Mexican concrete floor. We were quiet then too—reflecting, thinking, wondering about those we had served this week.

When we close our eyes, we see a catalog of Mexican faces—old wrinkled ones, young hopeful ones, faces with eyes clouded over with pain. What will become of them? Were they helped? Did we do the right thing?

The farmer who needed the strength and flexibility to harvest his crop—will the ibuprofen we gave him effectively relieve his crippling back pain? Will the prescription cream heal the swollen sores marring the 16-year-old's pretty face? Will the prenatal vitamins result in a healthy baby for the young, poorly nourished mother of three?

And how about the Spanish Bibles that we handed out? Will they be read? Were the sermons that were preached taken to heart? Will the children, the ones whose faces and voices reminded us of bright little birds, remember—and for how long—that Jesus really, really loves them as they are?

Tidy Americans, we like stories that have a beginning, a middle, and an end—a *happy* end, to be exact. We want to know that our actions bring about respectable results. Folks in our churches back home, who often help finance our trips, politely request numbers, details, outcomes. And we want them too.

The truth?

Rarely do we find out how much good any of our acts of service do. Seldom do we know the outcome of a particular patient, or of a particular situation, and only God knows whether our efforts have helped move hearts toward Him.

We know this—but still, in our silence we wonder.

Once we're aloft, soft drinks are served. Lunch too. There is to be a movie. Time for naps. Finally, now that we are actually on our way, we settle in, relax, chat, and eat. Seated as we are in the very back seats of the plane, Mom, Toni, and I are privy to all that's going on throughout the cabin. Folks with restless legs roam up and down the aisle. Babies cry. A hungry teenager requests a second meal.

It is Toni who first notices a disturbance several rows up. "Look up there. Wonder what's wrong?"

We watch while two, then three flight attendants attend a passenger occupying a window seat. Blankets are brought down from the space overhead. Someone offers a glass of water. As I crane my neck to see what's going on, other passengers in that same row are moved away.

Within minutes, one of the flight attendants strides to her back-of-the-plane work station less than a foot from where we sit. "Ladies and gentlemen," she announces over the speaker, "we have a passenger on board who is in need of medical attention. If there is a doctor or nurse on board who is willing to lend aid, please let a flight attendant know immediately."

I've heard those words on television, but never in real life. I look around, wait for someone with more training than I to respond—a doctor perhaps, maybe an advanced nurse-practitioner—but no one does.

"I'm a registered nurse," I tell her. "May I help?"

She directs me forward. The passenger with the problem is a man—little more than a boy really, only 21 years old. His name is Juan, and he speaks no English. At this moment he is experiencing some sort of seizure or spasm—I don't know what—trembling and shaking, feeling terrible, experiencing an odd involuntary drawing-up of both his hands and arms like I've not seen before.

With my limited Spanish and the help of a bilingual flight attendant, I ask the standard questions. "Do you have any medical conditions? Diabetes? Heart trouble? Breathing problems? A nervous condition?"

"No," he answers, not looking me in the eye. None of those. I notice the spasms have ceased while we speak.

"Allergies?"

"No."

"Do you take any medication?"

"No."

"Use street drugs or drink alcohol?"

"No. Only one beer last night." His eyes are afraid. He is pale. Again, he starts to tremble and shake.

Silently I pray: *God, please let him be okay. Please just let him be okay.* For here on this airplane, called on to provide care for a patient I don't know, who has a condition I can't identify, I too am terribly afraid.

But I don't let on.

"You are going to be fine," I say instead. Though he still won't look at me, I clasp his clammy hand—pat it—stroke it—hold it in my own. His shaking stops, and I recall my teenage daughter saying that she can tell when I'm nervous by the way I pat and rub. "I'm a nurse with years and years of experience," I tell him. "I know just what to do. I'll stay with you and take care of you until we land. Try to relax. Everything is going to be all right."

Because he's had nothing to eat today, I think that perhaps his blood sugar is low. "We'll try a glass of orange juice," I tell an attendant.

He takes the glass, sips a bit, then vomits into a bag.

The flight attendants bring me what I need: gloves, biohazard bags, wet cloths for his forehead, a CPR face shield to have ready should he stop breathing.

God, please let him be okay.

I help him clean up. He is sweating, but says he has no chest pain, actually no pain anywhere. I can't see that he's short of breath. *Panic attack?* I wonder. *Allergic reaction? Electrolyte imbalance?* These are only guesses. *How much longer until we land?*

"We have on board an automatic external defibrillator if at some point you need it," a flight attendant whispers in my ear.

"We *won't* be needing it. He's going to be fine."

God, please let him be okay.

Minutes later a different attendant approaches. "The captain has sent me to ask you if he should divert the flight to San Antonio in order to get the passenger to medical attention on the ground more quickly. It will save 30 minutes."

I look over at Juan. He's leaned back in the seat. His eyes are closed, and he's breathing normally. He's not moved, not had any of the spasms for the past 20 minutes or so. At the moment he looks to be sleeping.

"I think he's okay to go on to Dallas," I say. "He seems to be doing all right for now. I think he'll be okay."

"I'll relay that to the captain."

Left sitting there beside Juan, I begin to question my words. Did I say the right thing? What if I've made the wrong decision? What if he suddenly gets worse? What if Juan *dies* because I've told the captain to go on? My rubbing and patting intensify.

God, please, please let him be okay.

For the rest of the flight, I sit sideways in my seat, holding Juan's hand, watching his chest rise and fall, and studying the pulse I can see in his neck. I do not take my eyes off him save to look at my watch—which is obviously malfunctioning—for time seems not to be passing at all.

But it does pass.

First one hour.

Then two.

Only when the plane touches down do I release Juan's hand. He opens his eyes and straightens up in his seat. The plane taxis down the runway, pulls into the terminal, and finally comes to a stop, but we don't move. At the request of the flight attendants, Juan and I remain seated until the rest of the other passengers have gotten off.

Three male paramedics, who—alerted to the problem while we were still in the air—have been ready and waiting and anticipating our arrival, stride on board. Toting well-stocked medical equipment bags, looking calm and confident, they make the trek back to where Juan and I sit.

I greet the men, identify myself, and give them the details of Juan's episode in flight. They nod, take notes, and ask for a few details that I've left out.

"Thanks for your help. Appreciate it." They shake my hand. "We'll take over from here."

And, gratefully, they do. Yet though I am not needed anymore, inside I feel hesitant to leave. Slowly I walk up the aisle toward the front of the plane. The flight attendants and the captain watch me as I come. When I reach the area of the cockpit, they pump my hand and they thank me, and I try really hard not to cry.

Just before I exit, I take a long look back. I watch as the men check vital signs, start an IV, listen to Juan's heart. *He's going to be all right,* I assure myself. *You did the right thing. He's in good hands, and everything has turned out just fine.*

But I'm not able to convince myself. My heart hurts, and my steps slow, because I know that once again the situation is out of my hands. On this day, like the others, I won't find out the outcome of my deeds; I will never know for sure if I did the right thing, if I made a real difference, if my efforts truly impacted a life.

And so I'll pray—as I always do—for the Father to grant a happy, unseen end.

> *We are God's workmanship,*
> *created in Christ Jesus to do good works,*
> *which God prepared in advance for us to do.*
> EPHESIANS 2:10

CHAPTER TWENTY-FIVE

MOM'S BIG SPLASH

On paper, my driving record appears almost perfect. Behind the wheel for more than 25 years now, I've only received one speeding ticket, and I've never had a wreck—at least with another moving vehicle. True confession: What I *have* done is run into and almost crash through a wall in my parents' garage, twice back into a pole at Arby's, and three times dent the fenders of legally parked cars.

Each time I was so upset that I cried.

What can I say? From the very beginning driving has not come easily to me. I get nervous. My palms sweat. At 16, I failed both the written *and* the behind-the-wheel parts of my driving test—the written portion because I forgot to study, the driving, because I knocked down and ran over the parallel-parking pole. Lousy too at tennis and golf, I've often wondered if perhaps my poor driving is the result of some rare hand-eye-brake-pedal–coordination disorder. Surely there's a name for it. Dyslexic driving maybe?

Too bad. I live in Texas, a wide-open place where public transportation is almost nonexistent and where driving is considered to be a right as basic as life, liberty, and the pursuit of happiness. In the Lone Star State, taking one's rightful place behind the wheel upon turning 16 is an assumed rite of passage. So like everyone else I know, I drive everywhere I go.

Just not very well.

Which I suppose makes my several-years-ago choice to work as a home-health nurse, a position that involved traveling miles and miles—sometimes a hundred or more a day—seem rather strange. But oh, how I loved my job. Every morning, setting out in my little blue station wagon to deliver care to my housebound patients, I knew that I would enjoy experiences and challenges different from the ones of the day before. Speeding down interstate highways, creeping up muddy cow trails, turning into cute little cul-de-sacs, with my medical supplies in tow, come rain or shine I did whatever it took to take care of my patients.

When a nurse signs up to work in home health, it is with the understanding that she will go wherever she is needed, into whatever neighborhoods are required of her, to visit all patients assigned to her. She is expected to treat the rich, the poor, the critical and the chronic, to care for all people the same regardless of their religion, their race, or their age. The places where she delivers care reflect the demographics of the community in which she works. A home-health nurse's first patient of the day may be an elderly Hispanic woman living comfortably in a daughter's tidy split-level. Her last afternoon call could be at the run-down shack of a middle-aged, disabled white male.

"Doesn't it scare you to go into people's houses like you do?" I was asked more than once about my job.

"Aren't you afraid—driving through such bad neighborhoods?"

"Do you carry pepper spray?"

"Have you thought about getting a gun?" (Remember—I do live in Texas.)

Not really, I answer. *No. Never thought about it. Come on, you must be kidding!*

Truth is, I never did feel afraid. Unsure maybe. A little nervous on the first call perhaps. But no more uncomfortable than I've felt when visiting an unfamiliar church or arriving at a new friend's house for dinner.

At least that's the way I felt until I made my big splash.

It had been raining all morning. My second patient of the day, Mrs. Tucker, an 83-year-old, African–American diabetic, resided in the far east section of town. Her fenced yard was surrounded on all sides by other African–American families. As far as I could tell, no white folks like me lived anywhere around.

"Is that a problem?" my supervisor had asked when she first assigned Mrs. Tucker to me.

Problem? Of course not! What did she think I was—a *racist?* I didn't care what color a person happened to be. Black folks. White folks. All the same to me. Why, I was practically color-blind.

I'd been coming to Mrs. Tucker's house for several weeks, and not once had I experienced even a bit of trouble making my calls—though I admit I felt conspicuously pale. As I drove the narrow, poorly maintained streets, I received lots of curious looks and stares. Obviously, a middle-aged, blond-haired lady like me did not belong in this neighborhood. In response to the looks I got, I waved at people sitting on their porches, grinned at kids on their bicycles, and nodded at old men in their pickup trucks.

Most of them, after a moment's hesitation, smiled and waved back.

On this day, having just passed through a heavy spot of rain and feeling relieved that it had finally stopped, I was going over in my mind the tasks I needed to take care of during my visit with Mrs. Tucker. *Today's blood-draw day,* I remembered. *I've got to ask her if her feet are better since she started using that new cream the doctor gave her last week. Wonder if she's been taking my suggestion about having a light snack in the afternoon.* So deep in thought was I, weaving from one side of the street to the other, dodging puddles and potholes, that I didn't notice the four men bent over at work on the engine of a stalled-out car parked right next to the street. Nor did I see the huge puddle right beside them.

That is, until I hit it dead center and splashed cold, muddy water over all four of them.

Oops.

My hand flew to my mouth, and without even thinking I bore down on the gas.

Startled when they felt the water hit their backs, the men jumped, hurled curses at me, and shook their fists at my car.

I didn't blame them. Behind the wheel I was trembling, hot with embarrassment and shame. But what to do? Should I brake, back up, get out, and explain that I was sorry? Tell them that it was an accident? That I had not even seen them *or* the puddle? Should I try to convince them that I'm not, could not be, would *never* be the kind of person who would splash someone on purpose?

That night, over dinner, I told my husband and my children about what I'd done.

"Mommy! You mean you got them all wet?" Daughter Rachel was horrified.

"How could you not see them, Mom?" asked son Russell.

"You didn't stop, did you?" asked husband Randy.

I hung my head. "No. I kept on going. But I feel like I should have."

"Annette, you did the right thing," Randy said. "If those men were really mad there's no telling what they would have done. And if *I* were them and you splashed water on me, well, let me tell you, *I* would have been mad for sure!"

"Thanks a lot," I said.

"Maybe you should watch the street a little closer next time," suggested Russell helpfully.

Great. Just what I need, I thought, *driving advice from my 11-year-old son.*

Two weeks later, again I had a story to tell at dinner. This one did not involve water—or any other misdeed—but an interesting old woman to whom I'd given a ride to the store.

"Today I was driving down the street near Mrs. Tucker's house again when I saw this cute little lady—"

"Mommy!" Rachel's eyes got big.

"—she was wearing a pink hat and carrying this really big box—"

"Mom. You didn't." Russell looked stricken.

"Annette," Randy interrupted, "you didn't splash a *woman*, did you?"

"No! Of course not! I gave her a *ride!*"

Can you believe my family has so little faith in me?

I still endure teasing about the day I made my big splash. My children remind me of the incident just to watch me squirm. I know, I know. It *is* a funny story: Mom and her pitiful driving.

Yet to this day, when I recall the morning ten years ago when I splashed those men, I wince inside. I feel great shame. I hate that it happened.

How could I have been so preoccupied as to do such a thing?

What was I thinking?

Why wasn't I more careful?

In days past, when I heard the word *racist*, pictures of violence, hatred, and demonstrations came to my mind. I thought of folks in white hoods, of men with torches, of burning churches and burning crosses. Such repugnant images helped me feel good about my open-minded, charity-giving, liberal self.

No more. These days I find no assurance in holding such beliefs. The uncomfortable truth? The disturbing reality? I've come to believe that a racist is anyone who is traveling too fast. A racist is simply a person who is consumed with their own agenda. A racist is someone so fixed on their own destination that they never even *see* that there are people who are stalled on the side of the road.

The painful truth?

A racist may be someone who's exactly like me.

> *Jesus said:*
>
> *"A man was going down from Jerusalem to Jericho, when he fell into the hands of robbers. They stripped him of his clothes, beat him and went away, leaving him half dead. A priest happened to be going down the same road, and when he saw the man, he passed by on the other side. So too, a Levite, when he came to the place and saw him, passed by on the other side. But a Samaritan, as he traveled, came where the man was; and when he saw him, he took pity on him. He went to him and bandaged his wounds, pouring on oil and wine. Then he put the man on his own donkey, took him to an inn and took care of him. The next day he took out two silver coins and gave them to the innkeeper. 'Look after him,' he said, 'and when I return, I will reimburse you for any extra expense you may have.'*
>
> *"Which of these three do you think was a neighbor to the man who fell into the hands of robbers?"*
>
> *The expert in the law replied, "The one who had mercy on him."*
>
> *Jesus told him, "Go and do likewise."*
>
> LUKE 10:30-37

Chapter Twenty-Six

Poor in Spirit

When, three days after high-school graduation, I enrolled in my first semester of nursing school, it was with the solid expectation that I would learn how to give shots, take blood pressure, change surgical dressings, and start IV lines. That sums up what I thought a nurse needed to learn to do. I also enrolled expecting to get to wear a cute uniform, a funny hat, and ugly shoes. Both sets of expectations I'd gleaned from watching soap operas on TV and from reading oodles of "Cherry Ames" books when I was a little girl.

While I didn't miss the wardrobe mark by far *(What do you mean, my student-nurse uniform is supposed to come to below my knees? You're kidding—right?),* I was surprised to learn that nurses had to do lots of stuff I'd never even thought about.

Way before any of us students were ever let loose on real people, we were required to spend hours practicing on mannequins and on each other. That was sort of fun.

What was less fun was the requirement that we learn how to comply with the myriad of documentation details expected of a modern nurse. (As I recall, my old friend Cherry did not spend *her* valuable time on paperwork.) We learned to write Nursing Assessments, Nursing Care Plans, Nurse's Notes, Nursing Discharge Summaries, and more. Though all of this documentation was time-consuming, frustrating, and difficult to master, it was the Individual Patient Teaching Plan that taxed my brain the most.

Early on, I was taught by my nursing school instructors that any future hospital patient entrusted to my care must never leave the hospital without a clear understanding of his disease or condition, his prescribed diet and exercise plan, and adequate knowledge of all of his medications, including their schedules, effects, and side effects. Prior to discharge, my patient must also demonstrate to me an ability to make any lifestyle modifications necessary to promote optimum health and well-being. If this were not the case, it would mean that I, as a caregiver and health advocate, had failed at my job.

It was implied, and I blithely assumed, that all I had to do to provide such excellent care to my departing patients was to prepare stunningly clear Individual Patient Teaching Plans, present copies of the plans to both my patients and accompanying family members, and to post one in their charts. Also expected was that I verbally explain the contents of my Individual Patient Teaching Plan at the bedside and extract some sort of nod or intelligible murmur of understanding from my patients. The way I understood things, if I did so I could go home at the end of every shift at peace, confident that I had successfully fulfilled my duty as a nurse.

After finishing nursing school, passing my board exams, and being awarded the coveted initials "R.N." to wear behind my name, I began work at a large hospital, secure in the knowledge that I would be a good nurse. After all, during school I'd been consistently awarded high marks, especially for my Individual Patient Teaching Plans. No doubt my patients would be in good hands.

I loved nursing. Because I enjoy change, especially appealing to me was the wide variety of available positions. After working a few years as a hospital nurse, an office nurse, and a nursing-home nurse, I took an interesting-sounding job in home health. Working out of a local office, I would travel around and call on sick folks, mostly those who'd just been discharged from the hospital. I'd assess my patients' needs, monitor them for changes that I'd need to report to the doctor, and perform any necessary nursing tasks.

Should have been a breeze.

It wasn't.

At my new job I slammed face-first into the difference between what I and other naive hospital nurses like me expected of our discharged patients—compliance with their diet, exercise, and medicine regimes, for instance—and the realities they faced when they went home. What went on in my patients' homes bore little resemblance to the well-thought-out, neatly printed instruction sheets they received in the hospital. The realities of their lives required that I as their nurse learn to think outside the box, to come up with creative solutions to their health-care problems.

On my first day I met Leroy, a young man who'd been taught— by a well-trained hospital nurse I'm sure—to soak his infected foot in hot water twice a day. Leroy got his water from a contaminated well. He had no hot-water heater in his house. How exactly was he supposed to follow the instructions his well-meaning nurse sent home with him?

Mary Louise lived on Social Security—less than a thousand dollars a month. Sent home with five different prescriptions for medication, there was no way she could afford to follow the instructions she'd been given. One might assume she would have filled the most important ones—the two for her heart. But that's not what she did. Mary Louise instead filled the three least expensive prescriptions—a vitamin, a cream for a rash on her foot, and one to help her sleep. In her mind, she was doing the best she could with what funds she had available.

Tyrone was a diabetic of many years. When, on my first visit, I asked that he give me a rundown of his past 24 hours' food intake, he meticulously recited the sample menu on the take-home diabetic-diet sheet. Only after visiting Tyrone four days in a row, and each day listening to him report eating the same thing, did I catch on. Tyrone could not read or write, but he had a very good memory—such a good memory that, after surviving a dozen hospitalizations and listening to a dozen different nurses give the same discharge diet instructions, he had managed to memorize the entire sample menu.

Then there was Sal. Fifty-five years old and on disability for a reason I never figured out, Sal had been discharged from the hospital following a severe heart attack. Appropriately, she'd been sent home with instructions not to smoke, with orders to take her medicine, and with a detailed low-fat-low-cholesterol diet sheet.

On my first visit, after shooing a cat off the coffee table, we sat down together to discuss what she should do. "So, Sal," I said, "you'll need to start eating lots of fresh fruits and vegetables. Apples, bananas, oranges, carrots, tomatoes, broccoli. Which ones of those do you like best?"

She thought a minute, shifted in her chair, picked at a hangnail on her left thumb. I could tell that she was less interested in diet than in getting up the courage to ask to bum a cigarette. I don't smoke.

"Corn," she finally said. "I like creamed corn. Can I eat that?"

"Sure, you can. Corn is fine as long as you eat other things too."

"How about pork chops? Can I have them?"

"We'll need to talk about pork chops. They're not so good—"

"That's all I got to eat."

"Excuse me?"

"Corn and pork chops. I don't got nothin' else."

When I went to her kitchen, I saw that what she said was true. In Sal's pantry were a dozen cans of corn, in her freezer four packages of frozen pork chops. In the fridge I found ketchup, mustard, pickles, and a beer.

"Can you send someone to the store?" I asked.

"Nope. My check's all gone. Have to wait till the fifth."

Today was July the eighteenth.

"You don't have any way to buy groceries for the next two weeks?"

"No'm. But you said I could eat corn."

"What about your family? Is there any one of them who could buy you some groceries?" I asked. "Sal, it's important that you eat right—especially right now. Your heart is still healing."

She shook her head, wouldn't look me in the eye. "Honey, my family's poor as me. They don't got nothin' neither. Now you don't worry none. I'll fry me up some pork chops, heat me up some corn…"

I stopped at the grocery store on my way home.

Cruising the aisles for fresh fruit, fresh veggies, skim milk, whole-grain bread and pasta, brown rice, and skinless chicken breasts, I loaded up my cart. Knowing what I knew, having been blessed as I'd been blessed, there was no way I could let Sal go without. *Won't her face light up when she sees me coming through the door with my sacks of food*, I thought. Though the means to buy the groceries for Sal was coming out of my own shallow pocket (payday for me was weeks away too—and after this shopping trip it would be beans or bologna for my family several nights next week), and though if my boss found out, my actions would be frowned upon, her needs had touched my heart. I stocked up on three weeks' worth of what Sal should eat for her heart so that I could deliver it to her when I made tomorrow's visit.

When I arrived at Sal's tiny house the next day, I had trouble finding a place to park. Three cars and a truck had all pulled up into her tiny yard. *Company?* I wondered. *Something wrong?* I parked, popped open my trunk, and loaded my arms with her food. I knocked, and Sal called for me to come in.

When I opened the door, a cloud of smoke from the lit ends of half-a-dozen cigarettes hit me in the face. It took a minute for my outside eyes to adjust to the dimness of Sal's house. When they did, I saw that there were seven extra adults packed into her tiny living room. Though I had to squeeze through the crowd to get to

Sal's kitchen, not one of them greeted me. In fact, they hardly noticed my arrival, so fixed was their attention on a uniformed man working on some sort of wires or something coming out of the wall in a corner of the room.

"Company?" I asked Sal.

"Some of my kids. They're all excited because the man came today to install my new satellite dish. What you got in them sacks?"

"Satellite dish?" I set down my sacks.

"About time I got it. Living out here, it's a necessity. Why I can't get more'n two or three channels, less'n it's a real clear day. With my new dish they say I'll pick up more'n a hundred different stations."

I got my stethoscope to listen to her heart.

"Honey," she brushed me away, "I'm feeling fine. Really I am. Can we cut our visit a bit short today? The man's about got everything hooked up in there and I don't want to miss *Wheel of Fortune*."

A few preachers, some politicians, and many fine, taxpaying American citizens proclaim—with great conviction—that our time and especially our money should not continue to be squandered on the poor.

"Let them work like the rest of us."

"Have them learn to do without like other folks."

"They should learn to pull themselves up by their own bootstraps."

"Handouts don't do a bit of good."

I understand such views. People who say such things have, like me, been burned in the past by someone that they tried to help. Like them, I recoil at the welfare mother who trades her church food-pantry rations for lottery tickets and keeps on having a baby every year. I shake my head at the government-funded trade-school student who, upon graduation, elects to sell drugs instead of repair VCRs. I am frustrated by the rescued-from-poverty, fully-funded-college-scholarship recipient who does not even once show up for class.

The fact is, something that every person who tries to help must understand and accept, going in, is this—*the poor among us are not going to act right.*

Do any of the rest of us?

God offers us grace; we choose guilt.

He gives wisdom; we pick worry.

He promises us heavenly treasures, yet we spend days amassing earthly stuff.

We almost always do it all wrong.

Perhaps He—the Father—says to the other two of the Trinity with a sigh, *"They just don't act right."*

How blessed we are that He knew it going in.

You say, "I am rich;
I have acquired wealth and do not need a thing."
But you do not realize that you are
wretched, pitiful, poor, blind and naked.
REVELATION 3:17

CHAPTER TWENTY-SEVEN

PRIVATE TUTOR

It is Thanksgiving night, near twelve o'clock. Husband Randy and I, shoulder-to-shoulder in our crowded compact car, are into the second hour of our four-hour drive home, having spent this holiday with my extended family. Behind where I sit, our baby son, Russell, almost a year old, dozes in his car seat. He shares the back of the car with half a pumpkin pie and a quart of my grandma's cornbread-sage dressing. On the radio, John Denver sings of country roads while my eye-strained husband does his best to keep our little family in the right-hand lane of the one toward home.

Randy and I are good communicators. We rarely argue. Over breakfast each day, we speak of diaper rashes, discuss which bills to pay, plot the most effective way to approach our crabgrass problem. We plan our weekends and discuss where best to purchase a new tire. Like other busy young couples, in the daylight Randy and I confine our conversation to things both ordinary and urgent.

But we're not in the daylight.

In this warmth and closeness, surrounded by the hypnotic hum of the car's tires on the grooved pavement, in darkness so dense we are unable to read each other's faces, Randy and I speak of plans and dreams, of secret longings, and of hidden disappointments. Words cross our lips that we've not said before.

189

"You know," Randy muses aloud, "it's too late, and I wouldn't change a thing I've already done, but if I didn't have you and Russell, I think I'd quit my full-time job, go back to school, and become a coach and a math teacher."

He is only 23.

For a long moment no answer comes to me, only a trickle of secret, hurt-feelings tears at his unexpected revelation. *I thought our life was perfect. I assumed he liked what we have as much as I do. How long has he been wishing for something else?*

Finally, I swallow and speak. "It's not too late. There's no reason you can't go back to school."

"What about our house?"

"We can sell it."

"But you love that house and we've got so many bills. How would we live if I didn't work full-time?"

"I can work part-time. We can use what we make selling the house to pay things off."

"Really?"

"Really."

Even back at that young age, I understood that I did not want to be the cause of my husband's wish-I-could-have-followed-my-dreams midlife crisis. He should have the desires of his heart. I wanted that for him. And for me.

And so just like that we sold our house and packed our stuff. By the middle of January, a mere two months after that Thanksgiving discussion, the three of us were settled into a tiny university apartment, Randy was enrolled in school, and both of us had part-time jobs.

It took three years of sacrifice and hard work, but Randy realized his dream of a diploma, a whistle, and a mascot—a high-school team of his own. And though it had not necessarily been *my* dream, I happily settled myself into the role of supportive coach's wife. I bought the children (by now daughter Rachel had arrived) and myself T-shirts in the team's colors, learned his player's names and numbers, and baked frosted cupcakes for the team's kick-off-the-season Coke party. I believe I handled the adjustment to my husband's new career pretty well.

Until Carmen came along.

Within three weeks of joining his algebra class, petite, shapely, blond-haired, hazel-eyed, 16-year-old Carmen attached herself to my husband in a *most* unhealthy way. At least that's the way I saw it. Night after night, about the time Randy and I would get the kids put to bed so we could enjoy a nice chat, we would hear her knocking on our door. (We lived right next to the school.) Twisting her hair and popping her gum, Carmen would ask if Coach could *please, oh pretty please* help her with her algebra. It would only take a minute. She was sure of it. There was just one *little* thing he'd covered in class that she did not understand.

Yeah, right.

Randy never, ever told Carmen no—even though sometimes she forgot to bring her book.

While I busied myself folding clothes or puttering at the sink, my handsome husband and Carmen would sit knee-to-knee at my kitchen table, working on whatever lesson it was she didn't understand *now.* Hearing her giggle, smelling her heavily applied, musk-scented cologne, I would seethe inside. *Is he stupid or what,* I wondered. *Can't he see she's just using algebra as an excuse to be with him?*

For a while, I held my tongue. But finally, after Carmen's tenth tutorial visit in the span of three weeks, I could take it no more. After she left I declared in a haughty voice, "You do know that girl's got a crush on you, don't you?"

"Think so?"

"Come on," I hissed. "Can't you see that she just wants your attention? Don't you know that she's using algebra as an excuse to come over here?"

"Carmen never sees her dad." Randy's voice was steady. "He left her and her mother six months ago and he hasn't even called to see how she is. After he left, her mom took a second job working the evening shift at the nursing home. She doesn't get off work until after eleven at night. From the time Carmen gets home from school until her mother arrives, she is home by herself. That would be—what, five, six hours?"

I stopped my dish-drying and studied a dirty spot on the floor that happened to be near my feet.

"Carmen's brother, Marcus, who she's crazy about, left last month to go into the army. I know she's using my class as an excuse to come over here. I keep thinking, though, that if a kid craves attention bad enough to do algebra to get it, I should probably give it to her."

Ouch.

"But if you want, I can tell her not to come over anymore."

He means it.

What do I look like? Cruella DeVil? The Wicked Witch of the East? No way am I letting my husband apply for sainthood alone. I am one repentant wife. The *next* time that Carmen comes over I tell her how pretty she looks. The *next* time I bake cookies and give her some extras to take home to her mom.

And the next time I hug her when she first comes in the door.

That's the time that Randy hugged *me* when *Carmen* left.

By the end of this school year, Randy will have worked as a teacher and coach for 17 years. Along the way, there have been many Carmens and Carls and lots of other students he'll never forget. Randy has worked with kids who lived to play basketball but couldn't run, jump, or shoot. He once coached a special-needs kid whose mother insisted she play basketball though a blow to the head would be a terrible thing. Randy prayed and bit his nails every minute that the girl's feet were on the court.

When Texas instituted a "no pass, no play" policy, Randy began tutoring student athletes even if they weren't in his class. Over the years, he's washed stinky uniforms, bought road-trip lunches for kids who didn't have money, taken kids home after practice, and nudged pregnant girls to tell their parents *tonight* or else he would.

He has worked extra jobs to make ends meet for our family.

And through it all, Randy has loved being called "teacher" and "coach"—up until this year, that is. In a school that's weak on discipline and high on needs, he's now, after all these years, at the end of his rope. Tired, burnt-out, weary, and defeated.

Yesterday, I traveled with him clear across the state so that he could interview at a new school—one with high academic standards, well-kept grounds, polite students, and a supportive administration. After the interview, I saw him excited and enthusiastic—for the first time in months.

It's time to move on.

I know it.

He knows it.

But it's going to be hard. Moving is never easy. It's difficult to leave a place that you've grown to love as much as I have the dense forests of east Texas. But more than a place, I love a man. I want what he wants, so I'm praying really hard that he gets this job.

But no matter what happens, one thing's for sure: Randy can't stop teaching. After all, I've got many more lessons yet to learn.

God is not unfair.
How can he forget your hard work for him,
or forget the way you used to show your love for him—
and still do—
by helping his children?
HEBREWS 6:10 (TLB)

CHAPTER TWENTY-EIGHT

THE HEALING

Wearing blue jeans, purple flip-flops, and a bra, Candy Evans studies her reflection in the bathroom mirror. Self-consciously, she touches a place midway on her chest. "You don't think it looks too bad?" Born into the middle of a family of five girls, she is surrounded on all sides by helpful, advice-wielding women.

"No, honey, it doesn't look bad at all," a sister says soothingly. "But if you want to make it fade faster, put a touch of vitamin-E oil on it twice a day. It comes in a capsule. You have to poke it with a pin and squeeze the oil out—but it only takes a dab."

"I think if you were to put pure lanolin on it every day it would sort of *smooth* it out," another sister tells her. "You'll have to place a special order to get lanolin without anything else in it, but I'm sure Mr. Garcia at the drugstore can get it for you."

"Plain old Vaseline will make it less noticeable," suggests a third sister.

"Nonsense, all three of you!" interjects sister number four. "Remember, *I* have experience with this kind of thing. Sunshine is what Candy needs. Sugar, you lay out on the back deck with your blouse open for a few minutes every day. That's what I did to fade my tubal ligation scar. Look." This sister unzips her pants, motions for Candy to inspect her tan tummy.

As she's bidden, Candy takes a close look. It does look good.

"Can't even tell where they cut me, can you?"

After lunch, Candy shoos her sisters home—kisses them, hugs them, tells them all goodbye—and promises that yes, she will take their advice. All of it. She'll get some vitamin E, some lanolin, some Vaseline, and plenty of sunshine too.

That night, not a sister in sight, Candy and her husband, Robert, lie naked together for the first time since her open-heart surgery. Robert reaches over and turns on the bedside lamp. In the soft light, head propped up on one elbow, he reaches over and touches her scar, feather-light, with one finger. Until this moment she has kept it hidden from him.

"I know it's ugly, but I think it'll fade," she says.

Robert traces the snaky, raised red line from its beginning, just below her collarbone, down to where it ends, mid-belly. "I don't think it's ugly. Actually it's kind of cute."

Robert is a terrible liar, but Candy is grateful for the effort. She smiles.

His finger pauses at a place on the scar. "What are these little marks? They don't look like part of the incision."

"Those?" Candy raises her head from the pillow so as to look at herself. "Staple marks. They closed me up with staples instead of stitches. It's the way they do it now. Staples hold better and heal faster."

"Hmm." He rubs his chin. "Staple marks. I seem to recall some of the guys at work thinking that women with staples across their chests look pretty good."

"Robert! Don't tell me you've been looking at *those* magazines!"

"Me?" He's teasing her, pretending innocence, but the honest truth is that sweet Robert, though tempted, really *doesn't* look. "Why would I waste my time looking at some woman in a magazine when I've got you? You're beautiful."

He's about to get mushy. Candy can tell.

"Darling, the gals in those books don't have anything on you. You're every bit as pretty as them, and besides, now that you've got staple marks and a crease down your middle too…"

Candy giggles. "Robert! You are terrible!" She shoves his hand away, pulls the covers up, grabs at a pillow, and takes a swing at his head.

When, four months after her surgery, Candy is cleared by her doctor to return to work, the other ICU nurses and I plan a little welcome-back party. We divvy everything up and each bring something special—helium-filled balloon bouquets, fresh flowers, and a tempting array of heart-healthy, low-cholesterol treats. She's undergone a tricky triple bypass—an unusual operation for a woman like Candy, who's slim and trim and barely past 40—but her cardiologist has assured her that if she takes reasonable care of herself she can resume her normal activities, including her work as a registered nurse.

For the first few weeks, Candy's on the schedule only three days a week. Though everything is fine with her heart, she finds that she tires more easily than before and that when she is tired, things get under her skin in ways that they didn't before.

Such is the case on the day that Candy is assigned to care for Mr. Brooks, a 72-year-old farmer who has had open-heart surgery only two days ago. Though she provides professional, compassionate, and competent care, the rest of us nurses—Sherry, Layne, and I—can tell that Candy does not particularly like the man.

"Want me to take Mr. Brooks today?" I offer on Candy's second day assigned to the man.

"Thanks, Annette," she answers, "but I'm okay."

"Really—I don't mind. Remember when that woman with the gall bladder got on my nerves so bad? You traded assignments with me then. I could do the same for you today."

"I'll switch with you," offers Sherry.

"Or I will," adds Layne.

Nope. No matter how she feels, Candy does not want to trade. She can handle her patient *just fine,* thank you very much.

Realizing that keeping Mr. Brooks has become a matter of pride, we let it go, but tune our ears to every interaction she has with him—not difficult at all in the close quarters of our small hospital's cramped ICU. Still, throughout the morning, none of us hear anything out of the ordinary from either of them. It is not until after lunch that we learn what about the man is driving Candy nuts.

"He keeps trying to look down my shirt."

"Mr. Brooks?" Layne giggles.

"Sick as he is?" says Sherry doubtfully.

"Old as he is?"

"Are you sure?" I ask.

"Positive. Come help me change his dressings and you'll see for yourself."

Sure enough, she is right. The entire time Candy and I are working over him, Mr. Brooks doesn't speak, preferring instead to spend this time staring in fascination at Candy's V-neck-framed chest. I find myself oddly miffed that never once does he glance in the direction of *my* chest. As we work together to perform the multistep task, I sense Candy becoming more irritated by the minute.

"Mr. Brooks"—I seek his attention—"how many children do you have? Any grandchildren?" (It's been my experience that The Grandkid Question works 90 percent of the time.)

It does not work *this* time. Mr. Brooks ignores me and my questions but does finally speak to my friend. "Miz Candy, I hope you don't mind me a-sayin' this, but you shore do have a purty..."

Uh-oh. Here it comes. I hold my breath. Though I know Candy would *never* lay a hand on a patient, reflexively I reach out and touch her arm.

"...scar."

Sherry and Layne, eavesdropping from the desk six feet away, struggle to stifle hoots of laughter. They are only partly successful. I hear a snort escape from Layne, and from the way Sherry has her knees pressed together, I suspect that she is going to have to change her scrubs.

"Honey, you reckon *my* scar'll ever look that good?"

"Excuse me?"

The laughter stops.

Mr. Brooks reaches up and motions in the direction of his own tender, swollen, gauze-wrapped chest. He's still staring at Candy's partially faded scar. "I could tell by studyin' you that you had your heart operated on too. It don't look like it bothers you none. Don't it still hurt?"

"No, sir, it doesn't. Not anymore."

The old man shakes his head and presses his palm to his brow. "Right now my chest feels so bad that I wonder if I'll ever be up and around again."

Candy lowers the rail on one side of the man's bed. Moving in close, she takes Mr. Brooks's right hand in her own and guides it toward her chest until the tips of his fingers are touching the pale pink flesh of her scar. "See," she says. "It doesn't hurt at all. You can hardly even feel it, can you?"

"No, ma'am. I cain't."

And from that moment on—neither could she.

My heart is steadfast, O God;
I will sing and make music with all my soul.
PSALM 108:1

ABOUT THE AUTHOR

ANNETTE SMITH enjoys sharing her stories of faith and family, love and laughter, with groups of all ages. For information on booking Annette to speak at your next retreat, banquet, or other special day, contact Speak Up Speaker Services at (888) 870-7719; via fax, (810) 987-4163; via E-mail, speakupinc@aol.com.

OTHER BOOKS BY
ANNETTE SMITH

Whispers of Angels

Throughout her nursing career, Annette Smith has witnessed tender moments of caring and compassion, despair and doubt, love and laughter. *Whispers of Angels* is a heartwarming collection of "good medicine" that will bring you smiles of joy and a renewed perspective on life. Finding a good dose of humor and glimpses of the divine in hospital rooms and doctors' offices, Annette reminds you that life is a journey to be celebrated, and that in someone else's story you will find echoes of your own.

Stories to Feed Your Soul

This collection of delightful stories gathered across backyards and on front porches celebrates the caring, compassion, and craziness of small-town life. Filled with delicious discoveries and sweet surprises about the blessings of everyday existence, these tales of people just like us offer extraordinary glimpses of grace and goodness.

Help! My Little Girl's Growing Up

With big doses of humor and lots of practical tips, author Annette Smith guides you through the often tumultuous teen years when your little girl becomes a woman. You'll learn how to embrace communication with your daughter, deepen her Christian faith, and boost her confidence. Fashion tips, beauty secrets, and hints on how to provide emotional support will help you learn how to survive and enjoy your daughter's transition into young womanhood.

OTHER GOOD
HARVEST HOUSE READING

Beyond the Picket Fence
by Lori Wick

Bestselling author Lori Wick brings her vibrant faith and romantic heart to this delightful collection of stories about camping in the wilds, celebrating Christmas, finding "first" love, and more. These enchanting and lively snapshots of faith will capture your heart.

When Women Walk Alone
by Cindi McMenamin

Through the examples of biblical and contemporary women, readers will find practical, comforting steps for dealing with loneliness. Offers help in finding support from others, celebrating uniqueness, and gaining strength for single-parenting challenges.

Making Life Rich Without Any Money
by Phil Callaway

In *Making Life Rich Without Any Money,* readers will see glimpses of their own lives in chapters like "The Nearlywed Game," "Our Money Pit," and "Elvis and the Late Show." And through these stories, Callaway shows that the best things in life are not really things, after all.